BOOK SALE

Early Praise for *Build iOS Games with Sprite Kit*

This book is your quickest path from creating a new Sprite Kit project in Xcode to shipping an iOS game. Joshua and Jonathan have a great deal of experience creating games with Sprite Kit and teaching the technology in their popular seminar. In this book they show you the fundamentals and help you avoid the gotchas.

➤ **Daniel H. Steinberg, Dim Sum Thinking**

I had never written a game before, but with hands-on practice, this book guided me through the basics of how to set up a Sprite Kit app. In detail, it covers how to progress from the basics up to advanced topics, like physics, textures, and frame-based animations. This book is a great way to dip your toes into the exciting new Sprite Kit framework.

➤ **Ash Furrow, iOS developer**

Apple's documentation for Sprite Kit is pretty good, but it's not enough. Jonathan and Josh make it easy to understand the concepts behind developing games with Sprite Kit. Throughout the book you will develop two complete games while having fun learning about scenes, sprites, textures, and sounds. Are you building a new game with Sprite Kit? Just buy this book and read it.

➤ **Cesare Rocchi, CEO, Studio Magnolia**

As an iOS developer wanting to step into the world of mobile-game development, I really enjoyed reading this book. It's a great introduction to Sprite Kit, explaining the basics and the more advanced stuff very well.

➤ **Romain Pouclet, iOS developer, TechSolCom**

Rather than just telling the reader what to do, Jonathan Penn and Joshua Smith walk the programmer through why they are using a given method or set of numbers. Very few people go to this trouble, which is one big reason this book is a must-read.

➤ **Janie Clayton-Hasz, iOS developer at Digital World Biology LLC**

After reading the book, game development on iOS seems less wizard-like. I would not be surprised if there were a flood of games released on the market due to how easy the authors made it seem.

➤ **John Moses, developer**

This is a fun book! Sprite Kit makes it easier than ever to build games for iOS, and these authors know their stuff and know how to get you up and running with it in no time.

➤ **Kevin Munc, mobile developer and founder, Method Up LLC**

This book was so much fun to read and follow along with that by the time I was done, I had developed a solid grasp of the Sprite Kit APIs plus a fully featured game end-to-end. Well done, Rubber City Wizards!

➤ **Zak Nixon, lead software engineer and CEO, Deep Digital LLC**

Build iOS Games with Sprite Kit

Unleash Your Imagination in Two Dimensions

Jonathan Penn

Josh Smith

The Pragmatic Bookshelf

Dallas, Texas • Raleigh, North Carolina

Many of the designations used by manufacturers and sellers to distinguish their products are claimed as trademarks. Where those designations appear in this book, and The Pragmatic Programmers, LLC was aware of a trademark claim, the designations have been printed in initial capital letters or in all capitals. The Pragmatic Starter Kit, The Pragmatic Programmer, Pragmatic Programming, Pragmatic Bookshelf, PragProg and the linking *g* device are trademarks of The Pragmatic Programmers, LLC.

Every precaution was taken in the preparation of this book. However, the publisher assumes no responsibility for errors or omissions, or for damages that may result from the use of information (including program listings) contained herein.

Our Pragmatic courses, workshops, and other products can help you and your team create better software and have more fun. For more information, as well as the latest Pragmatic titles, please visit us at *http://pragprog.com*.

The team that produced this book includes:

Rebecca Gulick (editor)
Potomac Indexing, LLC (indexer)
Cathleen Small (copyeditor)
David J Kelly (typesetter)
Janet Furlow (producer)
Ellie Callahan (support)

For international rights, please contact *rights@pragprog.com*.

Printed in the United States of America.
ISBN-13: 978-1-94122-210-2
Printed on acid-free paper.
Book version: P1.0—July 2014

Contents

Preface

Imagine going back in time to visit the people who wrote for the original Atari 2600 game console and showing them games on an iPhone. Jaws would drop. Minds would be blown. They'd probably check for smoke and mirrors.

We've come a long way from the video game industry's humble beginnings. Writing games was a challenge back then. It still is today, of course, but the challenges then involved shoving individual pixels around, saving CPU cycles for rudimentary sounds, and interpreting raw player input from analog joysticks. Today, our challenges are often bounded more by our imaginations than by technical constraints.

And that's why we think you've joined us here in this book. You have an unprecedented amount of power in a computer resting in the palm of your hand. You want to write a game, and you'd like to do it for iOS. We have good news for you.

Welcome to Sprite Kit! Apple's exciting 2D-game development engine sports an excellent API to help bring your 2D game idea from paper to pixels. If you're already an iOS developer, then there's nothing else you need to do. It comes with excellent Xcode support and gives you a template ready to get started. It doesn't get any easier than this.

Sprite Kit provides the scaffolding for you to organize your game code, animate objects on the screen, play sound effects, handle touch events, simulate physical movements and collisions, and more. Any game that functions in two dimensions, such as platformers, puzzles, or overhead action games, will work great with Sprite Kit's tools.

This book will help you learn enough to take your own 2D game idea and implement it with Sprite Kit's building blocks.

How Do We Get There?

The best way to learn Sprite Kit is to build a game...or two! In this book, we'll walk through all the steps to build two actual games (that are quite fun, in the authors' not-so-humble opinions). We have chosen these games because they provide an opportunity to learn the way of the Sprite Kit APIs step by step.

Let's get to know these games.

Space Run

This will be an infinite runner game, like *Canabalt* but in space. The goal is just to stay alive as long as possible and rack up points. It's a single-finger game, which makes it a great fit for the casual game market. Check out the sketches in the following figure:

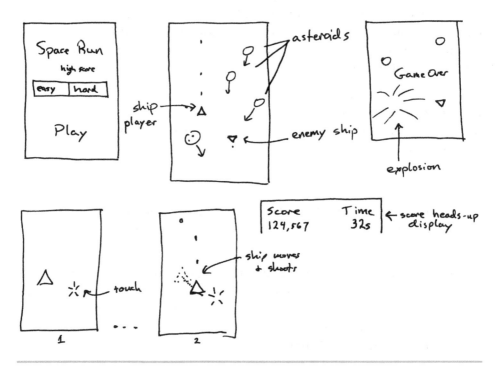

Figure 1—Paper prototype of *Space Run*

As the player, you are on a mission to race through light-years of space to rescue a distant science team that is in trouble. But this is no vacation cruise! You have to dodge things that will destroy your fragile ship (asteroids and enemy ships), and you can go on the offensive with your photon torpedoes when running isn't enough.

Here are the features we want to achieve:

- *Obstacles* - We want simple asteroids that just float aimlessly along a straight line, and we want enemy ships that spin and turn along a path to make it harder to avoid them.

- *Weapons* - The ship should shoot a photon torpedo at regular intervals. Any obstacle can be destroyed when hit.

- *Power-ups* - We want to give players something they can collect that makes their weapon shoot faster for a certain amount of time.

- *Variable difficulty* - We want to let players pick Easy mode or Hard mode, which determines the frequency of obstacles that appear on the screen.

- *Scoring* - We want to keep track of and show the player's score. Forward progress is difficult in the game, so the points awarded for each obstacle destroyed increase as a multiple of the elapsed time. Also, Hard mode doubles the point values.

- *Special effects* - What space game would be any fun without explosions? We need 'em—lots of 'em. We also need a thrilling deep-space star field zooming past to give the illusion of hyper-speed. The game should be a visual extravaganza of light and color.

- *Single-finger control* - We want this to be a casual game that's easy to pick up and play and doesn't require a lot of commitment to learn. The ship will follow your finger as you move, and the cannon will fire continuously as long as your finger touches the screen.

Space Run is perfect to start with because you can jump right in and practice moving a ship image around on the screen by handling touch events. You'll riff on the idea and add new features as you learn about them in Sprite Kit's toolbox.

Physics Ball

Classic pinball at its finest! We're going to build a simple pinball game with all the fun and physics of the real thing. It will be an excellent casual game full of sound effects and will automatically scroll taller than the screen. Check out the sketch in the following figure:

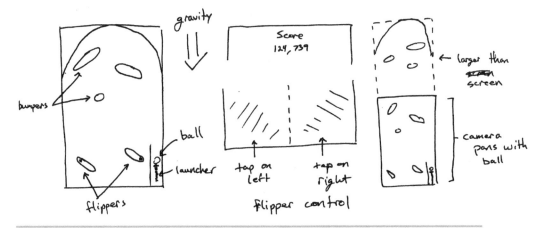

Figure 2—Paper prototype of *Physics Ball*

Here are the goals we want to achieve:

- *Physics* - This needs to feel like a real pinball table, with gravity, friction, ricochets, and spin.

- *Sound* - As the ball bounces around, we need to play sound effects. Lots of them. To protect the player from auditory boredom, we'll randomly pick from different sounds for each hit.

- *Bonus scoring* - If the ball flies past a special spinner, then that activates bonus score mode, and all scores are increased by a large factor. This bonus mode should be in effect as long as the spinner is in motion.

- *Camera panning* - The screen real estate on even a four-inch iPhone is kind of small.

- *Special effects* - We want to use little puffs and sparks whenever the ball hits targets or bumpers. All for the visual delight of the player!

- *Two-finger control* - A pinball wizard can play by sense of smell. For mortals the game requires two fingers. Tap on the left side of the screen to flip the left paddle. Tap on the right side for the right paddle.

The mechanics of pinball are well known, so this type of game will be a wonderful introduction to the Sprite Kit physics engine. We'll need to figure out how to handle collisions, define the shapes and boundaries, and control the physical properties of the ball in real time. We'll even make the playing field taller than the screen and add some "impossible" physics into the mix to make it more interesting.

This will be much easier to implement once you have the basics of Sprite Kit's APIs under your belt. You can jump ahead and dive right into these chapters if you want, but don't worry if you feel overwhelmed. This game builds on the knowledge from the earlier chapters. Take your time and enjoy the journey.

The Road Ahead

Reading this book is kind of like playing a game, too. You're the player. Your goal is to learn about Sprite Kit and have fun along the way. Each of these chapters is like a level, and each one has a challenge to implement pieces of the game as we've sketched it out. Here's an overview of the progress you'll make:

- Chapter 1, *Introduction to Sprite Kit*, on page 1, is our intro level—an easy one meant to introduce you to the Sprite Kit template that comes with Xcode and the simplest way to interact with a spaceship node on the screen.

- Chapter 2, *Actions: Go, Sprite, Go!*, on page 13, is the next level, where we play with more complexity. In this chapter you'll get to know Sprite Kit's actions, how to apply them to nodes, how to chain them together, and how to use them to help simplify the control of the spaceship and other characters on the screen.

- Chapter 3, *Explosions and Particle Effects*, on page 37, starts giving our *Space Run* game some sparkle and panache. We've got the ship, asteroids, and photon torpedoes flying around on the screen, but we want explosions to happen when they collide. We also want a thrust effect out of the back of the ship. Through all this, you'll learn quite a bit about the built-in particle editor.

- Chapter 4, *Menus and Cutscenes*, on page 53, is where we'll start stitching the *Space Run* game together. You'll learn more about Sprite Kit scenes, how they interact with UIKit, how to transition, and how to make an opening scene for your game.

- Chapter 5, *Keeping Score with a Heads-Up Display*, on page 77, adds some more visual feedback of the player's current progress through a heads-up display. We'll talk about laying out nodes where you want them on the scene and updating the game state throughout play. By the time you reach this chapter, you'll have a fully functioning *Space Run* game!

- Chapter 6, *Pinball Physics 101*, on page 99, is where we'll start building our pinball game. We'll start playing around with physics bodies in a scene to understand how best to model the pinball mechanics.

- Chapter 7, *More Physics: Paddles and Collisions*, on page 127, builds on the knowledge about the Sprite Kit physics engine and talks about collision categories, complex bodies and edges, and more to complete the essence of the pinball game.

- Chapter 8, *Polishing the Pinball Game*, on page 155, takes us deeper into Sprite Kit to polish up the pinball game. We'll build a bonus spinner target, frame-based animations to cue when the user should pull the plunger, and overlay table graphics, and we'll clean up some of the rough edges!

- Chapter 9, *Where to Go Next*, on page 177, brings the book to a close, reflecting on the games we created, the things you learned about Sprite Kit, and resources to go further in game development.

How to Get the Most out of This Book

Code is broken down by chapter and split up into different steps where it makes sense to take note of the code at that point. For the most part, you should be able to follow along and create all the pieces yourself on the fly. But if you want to double-check your work with the final product for that step or if you want to pick up in the middle, just find the appropriate code directory and start from there.

You can download the code from the book website.[1] Each code snippet mentioned in the book shows the path to the file where it came from. That will show you the chapter and step where you can catch up. If you are using an ebook format, then you can click or tap on the path of the file above the snippet to jump straight to the file hosted on the Pragmatic Programmers website. That makes it easy to cut and paste if you want to.

The book builds in *cognitive complexity*, meaning that the tasks you perform at the start will be very simple—just enough to get you started. It might feel rote at first, but that's because we don't want you to get lost in the complex possibilities that Sprite Kit provides later on. Each chapter assumes you've achieved the goals of the prior one.

If you think about, it's the same kind of progression that great games lead a player through. You don't know how to defeat the final boss when you first

---

1. http://pragprog.com/titles/pssprite/source_code

sit down to learn the rules. You need to feel the basic mechanics of the game, the way the other characters interact, and the boundaries of what you can do. As each step builds on the previous one, you'll discover how much you've learned when you look back at the beginning.

This is why we think it's best to work your way through the book in one straight go. But should you want to skip around (and we certainly understand the curiosity and excitement behind that if you do), then you can use the code checkpoints at different chapters and steps to catch up to where the book is at.

Expectations and Technical Requirements

This book assumes that you are at least somewhat familiar with the basics behind iOS development and Xcode. We recommend keeping these references handy as prerequisite reading:

- "Start Developing iOS Applications Today,"[2] an excellent starting place for Apple's official documentation

- *iOS SDK Development [AD12]*, by Chris Adamson and Bill Dudney

- *Storyboards [Ste14]*, by Daniel Steinberg

You should at least be familiar with Apple's introductory material, know about how view controllers and memory management work, and know how to build and run an application in the Xcode GUI. We'll be working with at least Xcode 5.1 and iOS 7.0.

Acknowledgments

We're so thankful for everyone who supported us while we experimented with the material in this book. To the CocoaConf team for the opportunity to run our one-day game workshop, again and again. To our workshop attendees, who gave us such great feedback. To Daniel Steinberg for all those deep lunchtime discussions when our paths crossed. To the Pragmatic Programmers for the opportunity to put our thoughts into this format. To our editor, Rebecca Gulick, for her patience and guidance. And to our families for putting up with the delirious antics of creatives under deadlines.

You've all impacted us. We hope we can do the same in return.

We also want to thank the technical reviewers for their work to test the narrative and code in this book: Janie Clayton-Hasz, James Dempsey, Mike

---

2.   https://developer.apple.com/library/ios/referencelibrary/GettingStarted/RoadMapiOS/FirstTutorial.html

Enriquez, Ash Furrow, Brian Hogan, Jeff Holland, John Moses, Kevin Munc, Zak Nixon, Romain Pouclet, Cesare Rocchi, Kim Shrier, Daniel Steinberg, T.J. Usiyan, and Miles Wright.

And now, let the games begin!

So, are you ready, player one? Shall we build a game?

CHAPTER 1

Introduction to Sprite Kit

Sprite Kit is an amazing little game engine. It comes with Apple's iOS and OS X developer tools, so there's no problem with getting started. With its simple API and boundless potential, you'll have your 2D game idea up and running on a real device in no time.

Let's begin our journey into the world of Sprite Kit by building *Space Run*, a single-finger game that's an excellent diversion for casual play and a great case study. We first sketched out the idea behind *Space Run* in *Space Run*, on page viii, so go back and refresh your memory if you are fuzzy on the details. Over the next few chapters, we'll build up this game piece by piece until we have menus, difficulty selection, scoring, cut scenes, explosions, and sound effects!

Apple makes it quite easy to get started with the Sprite Kit project template. It generates an iOS application with all the components wired up and a scene ready to use. We'll talk more about some of the underlying details of Sprite Kit soon. Right now we're going to introduce ourselves to the Sprite Kit world by writing code and pausing throughout to reflect on what we're doing.

What better way to get started than to figure out how to display and move a spaceship around on the screen in response to the player's finger? You'll learn how images are rendered as sprites. To update the position of the ship, you'll learn about touch handling in the Sprite Kit world and how the screen is updated for every frame. By the end, you'll understand how nodes and scenes work together to let you build whatever world you can imagine.

Ready? Let's go!

Setting Up a Sprite Kit Project

Start by setting up a new Sprite Kit project from Apple's template. With Xcode open, choose File > New > Project. Make sure the iOS application templates are selected in the sidebar and choose SpriteKit Game, as shown in the following figure.

Figure 3—Choosing the Sprite Kit project template

Name the project SpaceRun and set the device type to iPhone. Also, set the class prefix to the same as the authors' prefix, RCW. That will make it easier when you see filenames mentioned here as you follow along.

Run the app. You'll see Hello, World text on the screen, and a spinning spaceship node shows up wherever you tap, as you can see in the figure here. It doesn't do anything impressive, but hey, it's a template to start with. You'll want to design or buy graphic assets for your own games that you release to the App Store, but for now we'll just reuse the spaceship graphic in our game.

This template sets up a storyboard and an initial view controller that has an SKView instance as its view. This special subclass of UIView holds the entire Sprite Kit world, runs the game's clock, and lets us transition between scenes. We'll talk more about the SKView in Chapter 4, *Menus and Cutscenes*, on page 53, but for now you can rest assured that all the important parts are wired up for you. Let's get down to business and cover how to draw on the screen.

Figure 4—The Hello World program according to Sprite Kit

Drawing Scenes and Sprite Nodes

The template is a fine starting point, but if you're going to send the spaceship on a daring rescue mission, you need to figure out how to draw it yourself and understand what's going on. In this section, we're going to write code to experiment with scene setup and then talk about what goes on behind the curtain.

Start by deleting the contents in the RCWMyScene.m file that came with the template. Replace it with this implementation of the RCWMyScene class that displays the spaceship image in the middle of the screen:

```
01-SpriteIntro/step01/SpaceRun/RCWMyScene.m
#import "RCWMyScene.h"

@implementation RCWMyScene

- (id)initWithSize:(CGSize)size
{
    if (self = [super initWithSize:size]) {
        self.backgroundColor = [SKColor blackColor];

        NSString *name = @"Spaceship.png";
        SKSpriteNode *ship = [SKSpriteNode spriteNodeWithImageNamed:name];
        ship.position = CGPointMake(size.width/2, size.height/2);
        [self addChild:ship];
    }
    return self;
}

@end
```

Everything in Sprite Kit takes place within an SKScene object. Think of it like a stage where actors come and go. This specific RCWMyScene object is a subclass, and the -initWithSize: method is the *designated initializer*,[1] where we do all the setup we need before the scene is presented in an SKView and rendered on the screen.

We set the backgroundColor property to a black SKColor object. We then create a *sprite node* that contains the spaceship image PNG that came with the template. We update the ship's position property to be the center of the scene and then add the ship.

---

1. https://developer.apple.com/library/ios/documentation/general/conceptual/CocoaEncyclopedia/Initialization/Initialization.html

That's it! Run the application, and you'll see a huge ship in the middle of the screen, like the image shown here.

That's far too big. The Spaceship.png file defines a much larger image size than we need in the normal course of our game. But there's no need to shrink the image file itself. Sprite Kit is very efficient at resizing image textures on the fly.

Let's update the visible size of the sprite node.

01-SpriteIntro/step02/SpaceRun/RCWMyScene.m
```
self.backgroundColor = [SKColor blackColor];

NSString *name = @"Spaceship.png";
SKSpriteNode *ship = [SKSpriteNode spriteNodeWithImageNamed:name];
ship.position = CGPointMake(size.width/2, size.height/2);
➤ ship.size = CGSizeMake(40, 40);
[self addChild:ship];
```

Changing this size property applies an efficient transform to the pixels of the image to make the image fit within the given width and height. If you're familiar with the standard iOS Core Graphics routines, it's similar to what happens when scaling with a CGAffineTransform. But instead of calculating the transforms yourself, node objects expose simple property APIs to achieve the same effect.

Now run the game, and you'll see the image shown here.

Ah, that's much better! There's enough room for everything else on the screen.

What Just Happened?

Let's stop and reflect on what we just did. To draw the space-ship on the screen, we had to create an instance of SKSpriteNode and add it as a *child node* of our scene. The RCWMyScene object is a subclass of SKScene, which shares the same superclass as the sprite node, SKNode.

There's a pattern here that's important to point out. Everything that Sprite Kit draws on the screen is some kind of subclass of SKNode. Our ship is represented by an SKSpriteNode, which means that it is rendered as a *sprite*, or a textured image. The texture is loaded automatically from a file named Space-ship.png in this case. We're calling [self addChild:ship] to add the ship to the scene because our scene itself is also a node, and we want the spaceship to be a child node of the scene.

Sprite Kit uses this node tree structure to decide how to draw everything on the screen for each frame. In contrast to the way Cocoa and Cocoa Touch converse with you in their own flavor of the model-view-controller paradigm, Sprite Kit speaks the language of *scene graphs* to keep everything organized.[2,3]

Each of the nodes in this huge graph has important information about how the scene is drawn. Our ship node knows the texture that should be rendered, and it knows the size and position onscreen. Other nodes for labels, particles, and even empty nodes that are just containers for other nodes form the structure of the graph, as shown in the following figure.

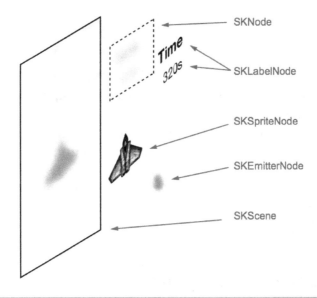

Figure 5—Nodes laid out in a scene graph

As our game evolves, we will use nodes of all kinds to represent the different characters that our player will see and interact with. It's important to note that in a scene graph, the nodes are both models *and* views. We're not in the familiar model-view-controller world that Apple recommends for normal iOS applications. We're in a scene graph. Nodes represent what is drawn on the screen, and they also represent the state of the game characters that change according to the rules of the game world. Nodes really are both the model and the view.

2. http://en.wikipedia.org/wiki/Model-view-controller
3. http://en.wikipedia.org/wiki/Scene_graph

Notice that strange text at the bottom of the screen that says "1 node 60 fps"? That is a special debug label added automatically by Sprite Kit. Take a look at the RCWViewController.m file in the -viewDidLoad method.

```
- (void)viewDidLoad
{
    [super viewDidLoad];

    SKView * skView = (SKView *)self.view;
    skView.showsFPS = YES;
    skView.showsNodeCount = YES;

    SKScene * scene = [RCWMyScene sceneWithSize:skView.bounds.size];
    scene.scaleMode = SKSceneScaleModeAspectFill;

    [skView presentScene:scene];
}
```

Don't worry about where this SKView object came from yet. We'll talk about how it relates to the scene graph of Sprite Kit later, in Chapter 4, *Menus and Cutscenes*, on page 53. The only thing we have to worry about here are the showFPS and showsNodeCount properties. Setting them to YES tells Sprite Kit that we want to see this special debug information to give us feedback about the load we are putting on the rendering engine. We'll remove these lines or set them to NO when we're ready to ship the game.

Our ship is drawn in the middle of the screen, but now we want to have it follow wherever the finger touches. Let's start working on that next.

Following the Finger Around

To move the ship around, we have to update its position property every time a finger comes in contact with the screen. Thankfully, handling touch events in Sprite Kit scenes is the same as elsewhere in iOS. We have all the standard low-level touch event methods.

We'll add this method after the -initWithSize: method to move the ship when a touch begins:

01-SpriteIntro/step03/SpaceRun/RCWMyScene.m
```
- (void)touchesBegan:(NSSet *)touches withEvent:(UIEvent *)event
{
    UITouch *touch = [touches anyObject];
    CGPoint touchPoint = [touch locationInNode:self];
    SKNode *ship = [self childNodeWithName:@"ship"];
    ship.position = touchPoint;
}
```

In the -touchesBegan:withEvent: method, we grab one of the touches out of the set with the anyObject method. Because our game is meant to be played with a single finger, we're going to let the system pick, just in case more than one touch comes in contact with the screen at the same time.

We then ask the touch to return coordinates in our scene's coordinate space using the -locationInNode: method and passing in the scene as the parameter. Remember that our RCWMyScene class is a subclass of SKScene, which itself is a subclass of SKNode. It's nodes all the way down to the bottom! Each node's children are positioned within that node's local coordinate space, just like UIView objects in normal UIKit. By calling this method with the scene, we are asking the touch object to convert from screen coordinates to scene coordinates so we have the right location to move the ship as the player expects.

Once we have the ship's new coordinates, we're ready to update the position property. But how do we get access to the ship node in this method? Here we're using one of the powerful features of Sprite Kit. We can give nodes names and look them up anywhere in the scene graph. That's what we're doing by calling [self childNodeWithName:@"ship"]. In this case, we're just looking for a direct descendant of this scene with that exact name. You'll learn how to find nodes with more flexible queries later.

Of course, to make this work we have to give the node the name we're looking for. Update the -initWithSize: method to set the name property.

```
01-SpriteIntro/step03/SpaceRun/RCWMyScene.m
  NSString *name = @"Spaceship.png";
  SKSpriteNode *ship = [SKSpriteNode spriteNodeWithImageNamed:name];
  ship.position = CGPointMake(size.width/2, size.height/2);
  ship.size = CGSizeMake(40, 40);
➤ ship.name = @"ship";
  [self addChild:ship];
```

Now, when we run the game, tapping anywhere on the screen updates the position property, and the ship jumps under the finger.

But we don't just want the ship to jump when a finger touches. We want the ship to follow the finger on the screen as it moves. Let's do that next.

Making the Ship Glide

As our game is now, we have a mechanical problem with our ship. It only moves when a touch begins on the screen, and we want it to move toward where the finger *drags around* on the screen. Because we get all the standard touch events from iOS, we could copy the same code into -touchesMoved:withEvent: and update the ship's position property there, but there's a simpler way with Sprite Kit.

Let's start with a property that keeps track of the touch that we received until the touch ends. Add this class extension to the top of the RCWMyScene.m file above the @implementation definition:

```
01-SpriteIntro/step04/SpaceRun/RCWMyScene.m
@interface RCWMyScene ()
@property (nonatomic, weak) UITouch *shipTouch;
@end
```

We're declaring the property as weak because we don't want to keep a reference to the object when the system is done with it. UITouch objects live and update themselves for the lifetime of the touch. The touch-handling system releases the objects when the touch is ended. Because our property is weak, it will automatically be set to nil for us.

Now let's set that property in -touchesBegan:withEvent:.

```
01-SpriteIntro/step04/SpaceRun/RCWMyScene.m
- (void)touchesBegan:(NSSet *)touches withEvent:(UIEvent *)event
{
    self.shipTouch = [touches anyObject];
}
```

Every time a new touch happens, we'll keep a weak reference to it so we can use it later. Next, we'll update the ship's position every time a frame is drawn by adding this method to the bottom of the RCWMyScene class:

```
01-SpriteIntro/step04/SpaceRun/RCWMyScene.m
- (void)update:(NSTimeInterval)currentTime
{
    if (self.shipTouch) {
        SKNode *ship = [self childNodeWithName:@"ship"];
        ship.position = [self.shipTouch locationInNode:self];
    }
}
```

The -update: method has special significance on SKScene objects. If Sprite Kit sees this on a scene, it will be called just before every frame is rendered to the screen. This is a great place to update the state of the game, such as making the ship node follow the finger.

In this method, we're checking to see whether the shipTouch property is nil. Remember that because this is a weak property, it will be set to nil for us by the touch-handling system when it releases the touches after they are done.

If the touch is still there, then we find the ship node by name and update its position property like we did before. Except this time, the position will change on every frame, and the ship will keep up with wherever the finger is on the screen.

It's great that our ship can move, but this isn't quite the effect we want. Our game mechanics depend on the ship gliding with a constant speed from where it is now to where the finger is currently on the screen. That makes it more challenging for players so they can't just tap around and cause the ship to jump immediately out of harm's way.

Smoothing Out the Motion

To create a smooth, gliding effect while the ship follows the finger, we'll want to update the ship's position to move closer to the finger over time, rather than jump right to the finger's coordinates. Because the -update: method receives the value of Sprite Kit's clock in the currentTime parameter, we can use that to calculate how far the ship should move by keeping track of the time between frames.

First, we'll add a new property to the class extension of the RCWMyScene object. We'll use this to record the last time we updated the frame.

01-SpriteIntro/step05/SpaceRun/RCWMyScene.m

```
@interface RCWMyScene ()
@property (nonatomic, weak) UITouch *shipTouch;
➤ @property (nonatomic) NSTimeInterval lastUpdateTime;
@end
```

Then, in the -update: method, we'll subtract the value of that property to calculate the time delta since the last frame.

01-SpriteIntro/step05/SpaceRun/RCWMyScene.m

```
- (void)update:(NSTimeInterval)currentTime
{
    if (self.lastUpdateTime == 0) {
        self.lastUpdateTime = currentTime;
    }
    NSTimeInterval timeDelta = currentTime - self.lastUpdateTime;

    if (self.shipTouch) {
        [self moveShipTowardPoint:[self.shipTouch locationInNode:self]
                    byTimeDelta:timeDelta];
    }
    self.lastUpdateTime = currentTime;
}
```

We're checking to see whether the lastUpdateTime property is zero first, because if it is, that means this is the first frame rendered of this scene. We need to initialize this property before we can get meaningful time-delta calculations, but we don't know what to initialize it to until the first time we are called.

Next, we calculate the timeDelta value by subtracting the currentTime parameter from the lastUpdateTime property. Then, if the shipTouch property holds a touch object, we call a new method to move the ship according to the touch point by how much time has passed. We're asking the UITouch object itself to give us the coordinate of the touch within the scene's local coordinate system. After all the work is done, we set the lastUpdateTime property to currentTime so we are ready to calculate the time difference of the next frame.

Let's write the -moveShipTowardPoint:byTimeDelta: method to nudge the ship by the appropriate amount for this frame.

```
01-SpriteIntro/step05/SpaceRun/RCWMyScene.m
- (void)moveShipTowardPoint:(CGPoint)point byTimeDelta:(NSTimeInterval)timeDelta
{
    CGFloat shipSpeed = 130; // points per second
    SKNode *ship = [self childNodeWithName:@"ship"];
    CGFloat distanceLeft = sqrt(pow(ship.position.x - point.x, 2) +
                            pow(ship.position.y - point.y, 2));
    if (distanceLeft > 4) {
        CGFloat distanceToTravel = timeDelta * shipSpeed;
        CGFloat angle = atan2(point.y - ship.position.y,
                            point.x - ship.position.x);
        CGFloat yOffset = distanceToTravel * sin(angle);
        CGFloat xOffset = distanceToTravel * cos(angle);
        ship.position = CGPointMake(ship.position.x + xOffset,
                            ship.position.y + yOffset);
    }
}
```

Yikes! If you'd like to take a moment to write apology notes to your high school trigonometry teacher, go right ahead. We did, too. Game development is a great way to refresh the mind on all the math we thought wouldn't be necessary in real life. Don't worry, we'll break down this code together. Figure 6, *Calculating the distance to travel this frame*, on page 11 provides a figure to help visualize what's happening:

First off, we are setting a shipSpeed variable to keep track of how many points per second the ship should travel. We find the ship node and calculate distanceLeft using the Pythagorean theorem with the ship's current location and final destination.[4]

Before we actually move the ship, we're checking to see whether this distanceLeft variable is greater than four points. If not, then we don't want to move the ship anymore. We're close enough. If we kept trying to move the ship anyway,

---

4. http://en.wikipedia.org/wiki/Pythagorean_theorem

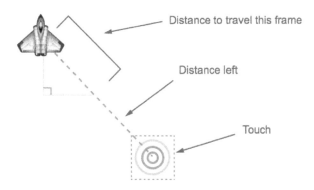

Figure 6—Calculating the distance to travel this frame

then it's possible that the ship would jitter around the touch point because of the imprecision of the floating-point calculations. Four points is far enough away that any rounding errors won't wiggle the ship around the destination point and close enough that the player will have the impression the ship reached the finger.

Assuming we're not close enough, then we calculate the distanceToTravel variable by multiplying the timeDelta by the shipSpeed. This is how far we should move for just this frame. We have to convert that distance back into x- and y-coordinates, so we use the atan2() function and some more basic trigonometry to set the ship node's position property.

Now run the game, and the ship will glide at a nice, constant rate to wherever your finger is on the screen. This is an important game mechanic because players will have to think about how to maneuver around obstacles as they approach. No cheating!

And that's it for our whirlwind Sprite Kit introduction! You've learned a little bit about how Sprite Kit draws things to the screen, you've learned how to track touches and update the ship's position over time, and you've learned about the frame update loop along the way.

This is a great start, but weren't we supposed to be able to shoot and dodge obstacles? Yup, and to do that we'll have to tackle the next topic, Sprite Kit actions!

CHAPTER 2

Actions: Go, Sprite, Go!

We've got the rudiments of Sprite Kit behind us. We know about nodes and the scene graph, how to display images with sprite nodes, and how to move the ship around on the screen in response to touch events.

Now we're ready for some action with obstacles, enemies, and a weapon with a power-up to defend ourselves. We're going to achieve these things with Sprite Kit actions, a powerful way to give behaviors to nodes that control what they do during the course of the game. By the end of this chapter, you'll understand the powerful building blocks for all kinds of complex behaviors.

Ready? Let's go!

Shooting at Asteroids with Simple Motion Actions

We'll begin by exploring simple motion actions that move nodes around on the screen. Although you know how to change a node's position in real time in the -update: method, which you did with the spaceship back in Chapter 1, *Introduction to Sprite Kit*, on page 1, we're going to use Sprite Kit actions to move the other nodes around on the screen. Any movement that is deterministic with a constant velocity works well as an action because we can just send the nodes on their merry way toward a destination point.

Before we start examining code, we need to make sure that the graphic assets for two new sprite nodes are in the project: the photon torpedo and the asteroid. Remember, you learned how to download the source code for this book back in *How to Get the Most out of This Book*, on page xii. We're going to begin in the 02-Actions/step01 step directory. If you've been building your own project while reading along, then drag and drop photon.png and asteroid.png into the file browser sidebar of Xcode to add them to your project. Make sure you have the Copy Items into Destination Group's Folder (if Needed) checkbox checked, and make sure that the SpaceRun target is checked, as it is in the following figure.

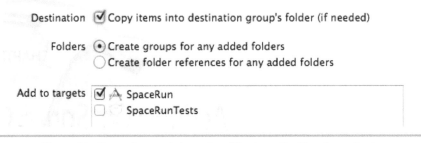

Figure 7—Dragging and dropping files into the Xcode project

Timing the Launch of Photon Torpedoes

Let's arm our ship with the very best ACME brand Mark III class photon torpedoes—an excellent weapon available at any fine retail space port. As we discussed when dreaming up the game back in *Space Run*, on page viii, our ship will shoot as long as the finger is in contact with the screen and steering it. Single-handed mechanics like this make it easy to casually play and will work great for our needs here.

To know how often to launch the photon torpedoes, we need to keep track of the last time we fired. Let's do this with a property on our scene object defined at the top of RCWMyScene.m in the class extension.

```
02-Actions/step01/SpaceRun/RCWMyScene.m
@interface RCWMyScene ()
@property (nonatomic, weak) UITouch *shipTouch;
@property (nonatomic) NSTimeInterval lastUpdateTime;
➤ @property (nonatomic) NSTimeInterval lastShotFireTime;
@end
```

We'll set this property every time a shot is fired and use it to calculate when to fire the next one.

Because we only want the projectiles to launch when the finger is in contact with the screen, add this code that triggers the launch inside the conditional within the -update: method that checks the shipTouch property.

```
02-Actions/step01/SpaceRun/RCWMyScene.m
- (void)update:(NSTimeInterval)currentTime
{
    if (self.lastUpdateTime == 0) {
        self.lastUpdateTime = currentTime;
    }
```

```
    NSTimeInterval timeDelta = currentTime - self.lastUpdateTime;

    if (self.shipTouch) {
        [self moveShipTowardPoint:[self.shipTouch locationInNode:self]
                    byTimeDelta:timeDelta];

➤       if (currentTime - self.lastShotFireTime > 0.5) {
➤           [self shoot];
➤           self.lastShotFireTime = currentTime;
➤       }
    }

    self.lastUpdateTime = currentTime;
}
```

We subtract the currentTime parameter from our lastShotFireTime property and check to see whether the difference is greater than half a second. If so, then we call the soon-to-be-written -shoot method and assign the current time to our lastShotFireTime property.

Don't We Have to Initialize lastShotFireTime?

Remember back in *Smoothing Out the Motion*, on page 9, how we had to check to see whether the lastUpdateTime property was zero before doing any time-delta calculations for movement? Well, we don't need to do that here. If lastShotFireTime is zero and current-Time is some very large number, then our ship will fire the torpedo immediately, and lastShotFireTime will be set to the current time. The timeDelta used for movement calculations is different because a very large timeDelta at the start of the game would make the ship seem to jump, which isn't what we want.

We know when to shoot. Now we need to make it happen. Let's write the -shoot: method that will add the photon node and send it off with a motion action.

02-Actions/step01/SpaceRun/RCWMyScene.m
```
- (void)shoot
{
    SKNode *ship = [self childNodeWithName:@"ship"];

    SKSpriteNode *photon = [SKSpriteNode spriteNodeWithImageNamed:@"photon"];
    photon.name = @"photon";
    photon.position = ship.position;
    [self addChild:photon];

    SKAction *fly = [SKAction moveByX:0
                                    y:self.size.height+photon.size.height
                             duration:0.5];
    [photon runAction:fly];
}
```

We find the ship node by name, just like we did in -moveShipTowardPoint: byTimeDelta:. Then we create a new SKSpriteNode with our photon.png image texture. We name it "photon" so we can find it later, and set its starting position to be the same as the ship before adding it to the scene.

Then we invoke the action magic. All Sprite Kit actions are created using class methods on the SKAction class. We don't need to initialize any special subclasses on our own; it's all handled for us transparently through Apple's class cluster mechanism. In this case, we're creating an action with the -moveByX:y:duration: class method and by passing it to the -runAction: method on the photon node. This causes the node to travel by the given y distance over the given duration of time in seconds.

In this case, the y-coordinate we want the photon to travel to is up and off the screen—far enough away to give the player the illusion that it just keeps going off into space. We're calculating that destination by adding the scene's height to the photon node's height.

But wait! Those who've been doing iOS development will wonder why we're *adding* to make the node travel *up*. In the rest of iOS, the default coordinate system has the {0,0} origin in the top-left corner, and y values increase for rows of points farther down the screen. Sprite Kit uses a flipped y-axis with the {0,0} origin at the bottom left of the screen, as you see in the following figure.

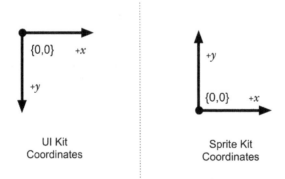

UI Kit
Coordinates

Sprite Kit
Coordinates

Figure 8—Comparing Sprite Kit and UIKit coordinates

Why? It's common for game engines to use this flipped y-axis, sometimes for historical technical reasons, but also because it resembles the Cartesian coordinate system used often in mathematics.[1] Just keep this in mind as you position and move your nodes around.

If we run the game now, the ship shoots while the finger touches the screen. But we can't stop here; we need to clean up after ourselves. All the photon torpedo nodes are left on the scene just above where we can see them. Sprite Kit is really good about ignoring nodes that aren't displayed, so we won't notice much of a slowdown for a long while. But every one of those nodes takes up memory space. We need to remove them from the scene when they're done playing their role.

Thankfully, there is a special -removeFromParent action we can run on any node to throw it away, and we can chain sequences of actions together. Let's change the -shoot: method to run a sequence that first moves and then removes the photon.

```
02-Actions/step02/SpaceRun/RCWMyScene.m
- (void)shoot
{
    SKNode *ship = [self childNodeWithName:@"ship"];

    SKSpriteNode *photon = [SKSpriteNode spriteNodeWithImageNamed:@"photon"];
    photon.name = @"photon";
    photon.position = ship.position;
    [self addChild:photon];

➤   SKAction *fly = [SKAction moveByX:0
➤                                   y:self.size.height+photon.size.height
➤                            duration:0.5];
➤   SKAction *remove = [SKAction removeFromParent];
➤   SKAction *fireAndRemove = [SKAction sequence:@[fly, remove]];
➤   [photon runAction:fireAndRemove];
}
```

We create the +removeFromParent action and then build a sequence by passing an array of all the actions to run in order to the +sequence: method on SKAction. No more memory leak! Now all we need is something to shoot at.

Plotting Random Asteroid Trajectories and Motion

Hurtling asteroids toward the spacecraft is a similar process to the way we move the photons. We just need to decide how often and when they should appear. Let's create a single dispatch point in our -update: method that rolls the dice and drops asteroids onto the scene.

---

1. http://en.wikipedia.org/wiki/Cartesian_coordinate_system

02-Actions/step03/SpaceRun/RCWMyScene.m

```objc
- (void)update:(NSTimeInterval)currentTime
{
    if (self.lastUpdateTime == 0) {
        self.lastUpdateTime = currentTime;
    }
    NSTimeInterval timeDelta = currentTime - self.lastUpdateTime;
    if (self.shipTouch) {
        [self moveShipTowardPoint:[self.shipTouch locationInNode:self]
                      byTimeDelta:timeDelta];
        if (currentTime - self.lastShotFireTime > 0.5) {
            [self shoot];
            self.lastShotFireTime = currentTime;
        }
    }
    if (arc4random_uniform(1000) <= 15) {
        [self dropAsteroid];
    }
    self.lastUpdateTime = currentTime;
}
```

We are using arc4random_uniform() to generate a uniformly distributed random number between 0 and 999. If the result is less than 15, then the game drops an asteroid, which is effectively 1.5 percent of the time a frame is drawn. Why 1.5 percent? It's just a number that seemed challenging enough while noodling around with different values. This is a great place to experiment and even make this number increase over time if you want the difficulty to increase as the game progresses.

Before we implement the -dropAsteroid method to actually do the work of sending the node down the screen, let's think through the math behind how we want the asteroids to move. The asteroids should travel at random angles and speeds toward the bottom of the screen. This is best done by imagining a funnel where asteroids randomly appear along the wide end above the top of the screen and travel to random destinations along the narrow end below the screen, as in the figure here.

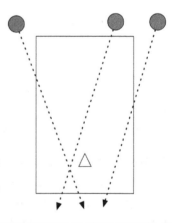

Figure 9—Asteroid start and end points forming a funnel

That means we need to generate random starting points, ending points, and random durations so our movement actions give the effect we want. Now we have enough information to set up the variables for calculations in the -dropAsteroid method.

02-Actions/step03/SpaceRun/RCWMyScene.m
```
- (void)dropAsteroid
{
    CGFloat sideSize = 15 + arc4random_uniform(30);
    CGFloat maxX = self.size.width;
    CGFloat quarterX = maxX / 4;
    CGFloat startX = arc4random_uniform(maxX + (quarterX * 2)) - quarterX;
    CGFloat startY = self.size.height + sideSize;
    CGFloat endX = arc4random_uniform(maxX);
    CGFloat endY = 0 - sideSize;

    // ...
}
```

We start our method by setting up the variables that we'll use to initialize the node and execute our actions. Let's walk through what each of these is for:

- sideSize—The value used for the width and height of asteroids. We're saying that we want a random value between 15 and 44. Remember, arc4random_uniform() generates a value between 0 and one less than the parameter given —29 in this case. We get the range we want by adding the lower bound, which gives us between 15 and 44.

- maxX—The maximum x value of the scene, the scene's width.

- quarterX—A quarter of the value of maxX. We'll use this variable to help the next equation make a little more sense.

- startX—The random starting x value for the asteroids. To get the funnel effect, we want to generate a random value from between –1/4 of the scene width to +1/4 of the scene width. That's why were using the quarterX variable and adjusting our random value to make sure it falls in that range.

- startY—The starting y value for the asteroids. It will always be above the top of the screen by adding the scene's height to the side height of the node.

- endX—The random ending x value for the asteroids, which is simply a value within the range of 0 to maxX.

- endY—The ending y value for the asteroids. It will always be below the screen by subtracting the node's side height from 0.

Phew! That's a lot of setup, but it's necessary to achieve the effect. We have our starting position, so let's create the asteroid node and add it to the scene.

02-Actions/step03/SpaceRun/RCWMyScene.m

```
// ...

SKSpriteNode *asteroid = [SKSpriteNode spriteNodeWithImageNamed:@"asteroid"];
asteroid.size = CGSizeMake(sideSize, sideSize);
asteroid.position = CGPointMake(startX, startY);
asteroid.name = @"obstacle";
[self addChild:asteroid];

// ...
```

We build the SKSpriteNode instance with the asteroid.png image, set its size to be a square of sideSize, and position it at the random startX and startY point. We're naming this node "obstacle" to make it easy to find later when we have to look up all the possible things that collide with the ship. And then we finally add it to the scene as a child node.

Our asteroid is ready to go, so let's construct and run the actions to make it move.

02-Actions/step03/SpaceRun/RCWMyScene.m

```
// ...

SKAction *move = [SKAction moveTo:CGPointMake(endX, endY)
                         duration:3+arc4random_uniform(4)];
SKAction *remove = [SKAction removeFromParent];
SKAction *travelAndRemove = [SKAction sequence:@[move, remove]];

SKAction *spin = [SKAction rotateByAngle:3 duration:arc4random_uniform(2) + 1];
SKAction *spinForever = [SKAction repeatActionForever:spin];

SKAction *all = [SKAction group:@[spinForever, travelAndRemove]];
[asteroid runAction:all];
```

The first action moves the asteroid to the destination random ending point built from the endX and endY variables we created earlier, and it does so over a random duration between three and seven seconds. The second action removes the node from the parent. The third action is a sequence of both the travel and remove actions.

For some extra visual interest, we can introduce a new effect by spinning the node at random speeds. The +rotateByAngle:duration: action rotates the node by the given number of radians one time. Because we want the asteroids to keep spinning, we wrap it in the +repeatActionForever: action so it will continue as long as the node is in the scene.

Finally, we want to run both the spin and the movement together. That's where the +group: action comes into play. We pass this method an NSArray of all the actions we want to run in parallel. Once we add this group action to the node, the magic happens!

Run the game, and you'll see the debris flying toward your ship. It might look frightening at first, but you'll quickly realize that you're in no danger. These asteroids don't do anything when they pass through the ship. Let's implement some simple collision detection next.

Checking for Simple Collisions

For our game, we want simple collision detection to check and see whether two node frames intersect. Sprite Kit makes this really easy. Let's start by calling a method named -checkCollisions at the end of the -update: method.

02-Actions/step04/SpaceRun/RCWMyScene.m

```
- (void)update:(NSTimeInterval)currentTime
{
    if (self.lastUpdateTime == 0) {
        self.lastUpdateTime = currentTime;
    }

    NSTimeInterval timeDelta = currentTime - self.lastUpdateTime;
    if (self.shipTouch) {
        [self moveShipTowardPoint:[self.shipTouch locationInNode:self]
                    byTimeDelta:timeDelta];
        if (currentTime - self.lastShotFireTime > 0.5) {
            [self shoot];
            self.lastShotFireTime = currentTime;
        }
    }

    if (arc4random_uniform(1000) <= 15) {
        [self dropAsteroid];
    }
    [self checkCollisions];
    self.lastUpdateTime = currentTime;
}
```

By adding this method call here, we're doing collision detection just before every frame is rendered. Now we can implement the collision detection by looping over all the nodes involved and checking for their frame intersection.

02-Actions/step04/SpaceRun/RCWMyScene.m

```
- (void)checkCollisions
{
    SKNode *ship = [self childNodeWithName:@"ship"];

    [self
     enumerateChildNodesWithName:@"obstacle"
```

```
    usingBlock:^(SKNode *obstacle, BOOL *stop) {
        if ([ship intersectsNode:obstacle]) {
            self.shipTouch = nil;
            [ship removeFromParent];
            [obstacle removeFromParent];
        }
    }];
}
```

We look up the ship node and stash it in the ship variable for use in our collision calculations. Then we use the -enumerateChildNodesWithName:usingBlock: method and pass it the name we're looking for and a code block that will be executed for every node that has the same name. This is why we named our asteroid "obstacle." Any other node that we want to destroy the ship upon collision will use the same name and will participate in this method call.

Inside the block of code we pass to this method, we are given two arguments: the SKNode instance that passes the name test and a Boolean pointer we can set to stop the loop, just like with NSArray's -enumerateObjectsUsingBlock:. For every obstacle node, we check for collision with the ship using the -intersectsNode: method available on SKNode objects. This does simple rectangular frame intersection, as shown in the following figure, which is sufficient for what we need now.

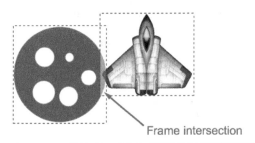
Frame intersection

Figure 10—Simple frame-based collision detection

If the ship and an obstacle touch, the game removes both from the scene and sets the shipTouch property to nil. This property is used by our shooting logic in the -update: method. If the ship is gone from the scene but the touch is still tracked, then photon torpedoes will appear to shoot from the {0,0} coordinate because the shooting logic is trying to look up the position of a nil node.

Run the game now. You'll see that the ship and colliding asteroids will vanish if they collide. That's great, but let's implement a collision check with our photon torpedoes so we can fight back. Add an inner loop that checks to see whether photon nodes intersect with each of the obstacles we loop over.

```
02-Actions/step04/SpaceRun/RCWMyScene.m
[self
 enumerateChildNodesWithName:@"obstacle"
 usingBlock:^(SKNode *obstacle, BOOL *stop) {
    if ([ship intersectsNode:obstacle]) {
        self.shipTouch = nil;
        [ship removeFromParent];
        [obstacle removeFromParent];
    }
    [self
     enumerateChildNodesWithName:@"photon"
     usingBlock:^(SKNode *photon, BOOL *stop) {
        if ([photon intersectsNode:obstacle]) {
            [photon removeFromParent];
            [obstacle removeFromParent];
            *stop = YES;
        }
    }];
}];
```

Inside our loop for each of the obstacles, we're adding an inner loop for all the nodes with the name "photon." Within the code block for that loop, we check to see whether this particular photon torpedo node also intersects the obstacle node's frame. If so, we then remove both and set the stop pointer parameter to YES to end this inner loop. We're stopping this loop because there's no need to finish going over the rest of the photon nodes to check for intersection with this obstacle. The obstacle is gone, so this inner loop is done.

And that's it! We have dangerous asteroids and a weapon to defend ourselves. Go ahead and play the game for a while to see how long you can stay alive. Seem too easy? Then let's add enemy ships that follow complex paths next!

Moving Nodes on a Path

Unlike the asteroids, the enemy ships should appear to be flying around. What we want is a way to specify a path the enemy ship nodes follow as they zigzag and loop around on their way past the player's ship. Thankfully, Sprite Kit makes that easy to do.

First, we need to add the enemy.png image to our Xcode project so we can use it in our sprite node. Drag it into the sidebar and set the options like we did before in Figure 7, *Dragging and dropping files into the Xcode project*, on page 14.

Next, we need to decide when to send the enemy ships toward the player. We've already established a nice random timing mechanism when dropping asteroids on the scene. Let's expand it by changing the section of our -update: method to call a general -dropThing method instead.

But What If My Images Are Not Rectangles?

As you're learning how to build your simple game, checking for node frame rectangle intersection is sufficient. But you may not get the effect you want if you have convex or very pointy shapes as SKSpriteNode objects, because the frame boundaries for the node might be far away from the pixels that the player sees. In that case, you can use the CGRectIntersectsRect() function to compare the two node frame rectangles directly and use CGRectInset() to inset, or decrease, the node frames to give the illusion to the player that the pointy parts of the node touch.

```
CGRect obstacleFrame = obstacle.frame;
CGRect obstacleCollisionFrame = CGRectInset(obstacleFrame, 10, 10);
CGRect shipFrame = ship.frame;
CGRect shipCollisionFrame = CGRectInset(shipFrame, 10, 10);

if (CGRectIntersectsRect(shipCollisionFrame, obstacleCollisionFrame)) {
    // ...
}
```

This code calculates new rectangles that are 10 points smaller (or inset) from the original node frames. Then, instead of asking the nodes whether they intersect with each other, we use CGRectIntersectsRect() to check whether the two smaller frame rectangles intersect. You can adjust these inset values to taste.

We'll also go over how to do collision detection with more precise shapes in *Detecting Collisions Between Bodies*, on page 144, but checking for rectangle intersection is fast and easy, and it meets the needs of our game for now.

02-Actions/step05/SpaceRun/RCWMyScene.m
```
- (void)update:(NSTimeInterval)currentTime
{
    if (self.lastUpdateTime == 0) {
        self.lastUpdateTime = currentTime;
    }
    NSTimeInterval timeDelta = currentTime - self.lastUpdateTime;
    if (self.shipTouch) {
        [self moveShipTowardPoint:[self.shipTouch locationInNode:self]
                    byTimeDelta:timeDelta];
        if (currentTime - self.lastShotFireTime > 0.5) {
            [self shoot];
            self.lastShotFireTime = currentTime;
        }
    }
    if (arc4random_uniform(1000) <= 15) {
➤       [self dropThing];
    }
    [self checkCollisions];
    self.lastUpdateTime = currentTime;
}
```

Instead of calling -dropAsteroid, we're calling the -dropThing method, which we build to choose whether to drop an enemy ship or an asteroid given a certain probability.

02-Actions/step05/SpaceRun/RCWMyScene.m
```
- (void)dropThing {
    u_int32_t dice = arc4random_uniform(100);
    if (dice < 15) {
        [self dropEnemyShip];
    } else {
        [self dropAsteroid];
    }
}
```

Remember that the arc4random_uniform() function returns a uniformly random integer from 0 to the upper bound parameter. The game reads this if statement to mean that an enemy ship will be dropped onto the scene 15 percent of the time; otherwise, an asteroid will drop. This method is now the key place to play with the probabilities of all the things that interact with the player. We'll tweak this more soon.

The -dropAsteroid method is already done. Let's begin to implement the -dropEnemyShip method next.

02-Actions/step05/SpaceRun/RCWMyScene.m
```
- (void)dropEnemyShip {
    CGFloat sideSize = 30;
    CGFloat startX = arc4random_uniform(self.size.width-40) + 20;
    CGFloat startY = self.size.height + sideSize;
    SKSpriteNode *enemy = [SKSpriteNode spriteNodeWithImageNamed:@"enemy"];
    enemy.size = CGSizeMake(sideSize, sideSize);
    enemy.position = CGPointMake(startX, startY);
    enemy.name = @"obstacle";
    [self addChild:enemy];
    // ...
}
```

As with our asteroids before, we're choosing a random starting point on the screen. In this case, we want it to start anywhere at the top, within 20-pixel margins on either side. We create the enemy ship SKSpriteNode, position it, and name it "obstacle" like we did with our asteroid nodes.

To make the node move, Sprite Kit gives us a special action that will follow a *Bézier curve*,[2] a kind of mathematical equation that uses control points to define how the curve of the path is formed. Here's an image illustrating the curve we want the ship to follow:

---

2.   http://en.wikipedia.org/wiki/Bezier_curve

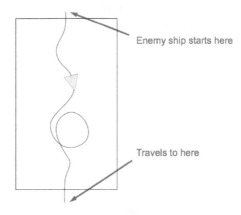

Enemy ship starts here

Travels to here

Figure 11—The path an enemy ship travels

We'll get to how we construct this path in a moment. For now, let's assume we can call a method, -buildEnemyShipMovementPath, that will return the path we want. We then create the path-following action and run it on the enemy ship.

02-Actions/step05/SpaceRun/RCWMyScene.m
```
// ...
CGPathRef shipPath = [self buildEnemyShipMovementPath];
SKAction *followPath = [SKAction followPath:shipPath
                                    asOffset:YES
                                 orientToPath:YES
                                    duration:7];
SKAction *remove = [SKAction removeFromParent];
SKAction *all = [SKAction sequence:@[followPath, remove]];
[enemy runAction:all];
```

The -followPath:asOffset:orientToPath:duration takes four arguments. The first is a CGPathRef, a Core Graphics data structure that holds the definition of the Bézier curve we'll create in a moment.

The second parameter, asOffset, lets us treat the actual point values of the path as offsets from the node's starting points or absolute positions on the screen. We're passing in YES because we don't want the points of our path to be interpreted absolutely. We're setting the starting point of this ship randomly and want the path to be interpreted as offsets treating the starting point as the origin.

The third parameter, orientToPath:, is the most beautiful part of Sprite Kit's path-following action. By passing in YES, the enemy ship will turn to face the direction of the path automatically. If you've ever tried to do this on your own in other game frameworks, you're certainly shedding tears of joy right now.

And the fourth parameter, duration, is the same as with all the other time-based actions we've used. We're saying that the ship should move over the course of seven seconds, following the path as an offset from its starting point, and orient itself to face the direction the path is currently pointing.

We then build a -removeFromParent action, join these two actions together in a sequence action, and finally run that on the enemy ship.

Creating CGPathRefs with PaintCode

So, we've put off the discussion about where this CGPathRef comes from for long enough. Let's implement the -buildEnemyShipMovementPath method and return the proper shape that describes the path our enemy ship will follow.

```
02-Actions/step05/SpaceRun/RCWMyScene.m
- (CGPathRef)buildEnemyShipMovementPath
{
    UIBezierPath* bezierPath = [UIBezierPath bezierPath];
    [bezierPath moveToPoint: CGPointMake(0.5, -0.5)];
    [bezierPath addCurveToPoint: CGPointMake(-2.5, -59.5)
                  controlPoint1: CGPointMake(0.5, -0.5)
                  controlPoint2: CGPointMake(4.55, -29.48)];
    [bezierPath addCurveToPoint: CGPointMake(-27.5, -154.5)
                  controlPoint1: CGPointMake(-9.55, -89.52)
                  controlPoint2: CGPointMake(-43.32, -115.43)];
    [bezierPath addCurveToPoint: CGPointMake(30.5, -243.5)
                  controlPoint1: CGPointMake(-11.68, -193.57)
                  controlPoint2: CGPointMake(17.28, -186.95)];
    [bezierPath addCurveToPoint: CGPointMake(-52.5, -379.5)
                  controlPoint1: CGPointMake(43.72, -300.05)
                  controlPoint2: CGPointMake(-47.71, -335.76)];
    [bezierPath addCurveToPoint: CGPointMake(54.5, -449.5)
                  controlPoint1: CGPointMake(-57.29, -423.24)
                  controlPoint2: CGPointMake(-8.14, -482.45)];
    [bezierPath addCurveToPoint: CGPointMake(-5.5, -348.5)
                  controlPoint1: CGPointMake(117.14, -416.55)
                  controlPoint2: CGPointMake(52.25, -308.62)];
    [bezierPath addCurveToPoint: CGPointMake(10.5, -494.5)
                  controlPoint1: CGPointMake(-63.25, -388.38)
                  controlPoint2: CGPointMake(-14.48, -457.43)];
    [bezierPath addCurveToPoint: CGPointMake(0.5, -559.5)
                  controlPoint1: CGPointMake(23.74, -514.16)
                  controlPoint2: CGPointMake(6.93, -537.57)];
    [bezierPath addCurveToPoint: CGPointMake(-2.5, -644.5)
                  controlPoint1: CGPointMake(-5.2, -578.93)
                  controlPoint2: CGPointMake(-2.5, -644.5)];

    return bezierPath.CGPath;
}
```

Phew! Yes, that's a lot of Objective-C code. We're using Apple's UIBezierPath class to construct an object that adds point after point to build the path, and specifies control points along the way that curve the line segments according to the Bézier curve rules. Once constructed, we call the CGPath property to retrieve the necessary CGPathRef structure and return it from the method.

Don't worry, though; there's no need to be a Bézier curve maven. Many tools out there today will let you draw shapes by hand and give you the Objective-C code that you need. For this particular path, PaintCode was used to draw and copy the source you see in the -buildEnemyShipMovementPath method. PaintCode is a marvelous standalone application that does far more than convert drawings into code.[3] You can import Photoshop PSD files and export complete Core Graphics drawing routines to drop right into a UIView, if you wish. Because we're in Sprite Kit, we're not drawing with Core Graphics, but we can still use PaintCode to generate the Objective-C for just a UIBezierPath object.

In the 02-Actions/step05/assets directory, you'll find the enemypath.pcvd file, which is the PaintCode file used to generate the path. It has a custom origin with a flipped y-axis to match Sprite Kit's coordinate system, and the origin is set to be the top middle of the canvas, as shown in Figure 12, *Building a Bézier curve with PaintCode*, on page 29.

This isn't supposed to be a thorough tutorial on Bézier curves or PaintCode. It's just enough to show you a simple way to build Bézier curves with a visual tool and use them. If you want, you can make up several curves and then choose between them in the -buildEnemyShipMovementPath method based on whatever rules suit your needs. Bézier curves pop up in other places in Sprite Kit, such as in the physics engine and SKShapeNode objects, so having a tool like PaintCode will come in handy.

SKAction objects provide excellent building blocks for all sorts of enemies and challenges. Just send the nodes on their way, check for collisions, and have them clean themselves up when they are finished.

But Sprite Kit actions aren't just for visual effects. While we provide a great challenge for the player, the experience is a bit bland. We need the excitement of sound effects, which we'll add next!

Playing Sound Effects in the Scene

When you're ready to implement one-shot sound effects in your game, there's no need to reach for the iOS audio APIs. Sprite Kit gives us everything we

---

3. http://www.paintcodeapp.com

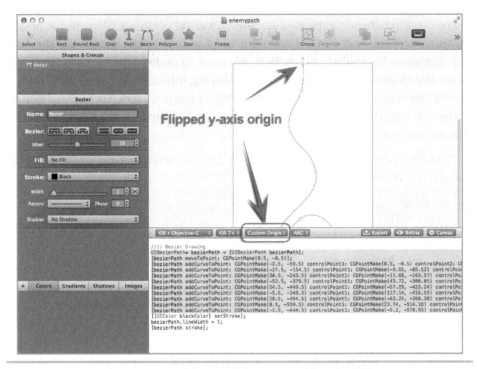

Figure 12—Building a Bézier curve with PaintCode

need with a special sound action. Let's add some shooting and explosion effects for the collisions.

First, we need to make sure the sound files are in the Xcode project. If you're creating the project yourself on the fly, drag the obstacleExplode.m4a, shipExplode.m4a, and shoot.m4a files into the Xcode file sidebar. Make sure the SpaceRun target checkbox is checked, like in Figure 7, *Dragging and dropping files into the Xcode project*, on page 14. Xcode doesn't always check that box for you for some file types.

Next, we need three properties on our scene object to hold the sound actions. Let's add these property definitions to the class extension of RCWMyScene.m.

```
02-Actions/step06/SpaceRun/RCWMyScene.m
@interface RCWMyScene ()
@property (nonatomic, weak) UITouch *shipTouch;
@property (nonatomic) NSTimeInterval lastUpdateTime;
@property (nonatomic) NSTimeInterval lastShotFireTime;
➤ @property (nonatomic, strong) SKAction *shootSound;
➤ @property (nonatomic, strong) SKAction *shipExplodeSound;
➤ @property (nonatomic, strong) SKAction *obstacleExplodeSound;
@end
```

We're creating these properties because loading a sound file into an action takes a moment and can introduce a brief pause in the gameplay the first time the sound is loaded and cached. We want to preload the sounds ourselves to get the delay out of the way up front during initialization, and we'll keep a strong reference to the actions so they aren't purged from Sprite Kit's sound cache for any reason. We know we always need these sounds available for this scene.

With the properties in place, create the sound actions and assign them to the properties in the -initWithSize: method.

```
02-Actions/step06/SpaceRun/RCWMyScene.m
- (id)initWithSize:(CGSize)size
{
    if (self = [super initWithSize:size]) {
        self.backgroundColor = [SKColor blackColor];
        NSString *name = @"Spaceship.png";
        SKSpriteNode *ship = [SKSpriteNode spriteNodeWithImageNamed:name];
        ship.position = CGPointMake(size.width/2, size.height/2);
        ship.size = CGSizeMake(40, 40);
        ship.name = @"ship";
        [self addChild:ship];

➤        self.shootSound =
➤            [SKAction playSoundFileNamed:@"shoot.m4a" waitForCompletion:NO];
➤        self.obstacleExplodeSound =
➤            [SKAction playSoundFileNamed:@"obstacleExplode.m4a"
➤                          waitForCompletion:NO];
➤        self.shipExplodeSound =
➤            [SKAction playSoundFileNamed:@"shipExplode.m4a" waitForCompletion:NO];
    }
    return self;
}
```

The -playSoundFileName:waitForCompletion: method takes a name for a sound file in the bundle for the first parameter. This can be any file that the iOS sound APIs understand, such as MP3, M4A, AIF, CAF, WAV, and more. While there are performance considerations when choosing sound-file types for the low-level iOS APIs, we don't have to worry about that for short one-shot sounds. M4A files are small, high quality, and quite sufficient for our use.

Notice how we set the waitForCompletion: parameter to NO for all these actions. This controls how the action fits in with the rest of the actions playing on the node. In this particular case, it doesn't really matter because we're just playing the sounds by themselves. But if they were part of an action sequence, then setting waitForCompletion: to YES would pause the sequence until the sound file stopped playing. That can be useful if you are chaining sounds together one after the other for effect. But for self-contained sound actions like this, we set the parameter to NO so that Sprite Kit knows we just want to trigger the sound and move on immediately.

With the sound actions initialized and ready to go, we'll add two lines to our -checkCollisions method to run the sound actions on the scene when either the ship or an obstacle explodes.

02-Actions/step06/SpaceRun/RCWMyScene.m
```
[self
 enumerateChildNodesWithName:@"obstacle"
 usingBlock:^(SKNode *obstacle, BOOL *stop) {
    if ([ship intersectsNode:obstacle]) {
        self.shipTouch = nil;
        [ship removeFromParent];
        [obstacle removeFromParent];
        [self runAction:self.shipExplodeSound];
    }
    [self
     enumerateChildNodesWithName:@"photon"
     usingBlock:^(SKNode *photon, BOOL *stop) {
        if ([photon intersectsNode:obstacle]) {
            [photon removeFromParent];
            [obstacle removeFromParent];
            [self runAction:self.obstacleExplodeSound];
            *stop = YES;
        }
    }];
}];
```

We're passing the sound action we want to play to the -runAction: method on the scene. That's all it takes to play a sound!

Notice that we're playing the sounds on the scene itself, and not on the other nodes. That's because we're removing those nodes from the scene, and any node that doesn't belong on an active scene doesn't run its actions.

Let's do the same thing to play a sound every time we shoot our photon torpedoes.

02-Actions/step06/SpaceRun/RCWMyScene.m
```
- (void)shoot
{
    SKNode *ship = [self childNodeWithName:@"ship"];

    SKSpriteNode *photon = [SKSpriteNode spriteNodeWithImageNamed:@"photon"];
    photon.name = @"photon";
    photon.position = ship.position;

    [self addChild:photon];
```

```
    SKAction *fly = [SKAction moveByX:0
                                   y:self.size.height+photon.size.height
                             duration:0.5];
    SKAction *remove = [SKAction removeFromParent];
    SKAction *fireAndRemove = [SKAction sequence:@[fly, remove]];
    [photon runAction:fireAndRemove];

➤   [self runAction:self.shootSound];
}
```

We're passing the sound action stored in the self.shootSound property to the -runAction: method on the scene.

Playing simple one-shot sounds is so easy with Sprite Kit. You can find out more about supported file formats in Apple's documentation.[4]

You're almost finished learning about node actions. For our last trick, we'll implement power-ups for the player's weapon.

Implementing Weapon Power-Ups with Actions

To finish out this chapter, we'll give the player a power-up advantage to help him clear a path through the obstacles. If the player collects the power-up, the ship shoots faster for a short time. Collect more power-ups, and the timer keeps resetting to give more time. Sprite Kit's code-block actions make this sequence of steps easy to do.

First, we need our power-up sprite texture, so drag powerup.png into the Xcode sidebar and make sure it is added to the target, as you did in Figure 7, *Dragging and dropping files into the Xcode project*, on page 14.

Next, we need to create a property that we will use to keep track of the current firing rate.

02-Actions/step07/SpaceRun/RCWMyScene.m
```
@interface RCWMyScene ()

@property (nonatomic, weak) UITouch *shipTouch;
@property (nonatomic) NSTimeInterval lastUpdateTime;
@property (nonatomic) NSTimeInterval lastShotFireTime;
➤ @property (nonatomic) CGFloat shipFireRate;

@property (nonatomic, strong) SKAction *shootSound;
@property (nonatomic, strong) SKAction *shipExplodeSound;
@property (nonatomic, strong) SKAction *obstacleExplodeSound;
@end
```

---

4. https://developer.apple.com/library/ios/documentation/AudioVideo/Conceptual/MultimediaPG/UsingAudio/UsingAudio.html

This shipFireRate property will be altered when the player collects a power-up and restored after the power-up timer runs out. Let's initialize this property in the -initWithSize: method.

02-Actions/step07/SpaceRun/RCWMyScene.m
```
self.shipFireRate = 0.5;
```

We're setting it to 0.5 photons per second because that's what we originally started with when we first wrote the -update: method to calculate when to shoot. Let's update that method so it uses this property instead of the hard-coded value.

02-Actions/step07/SpaceRun/RCWMyScene.m
```
➤ if (currentTime - self.lastShotFireTime > self.shipFireRate) {
      [self shoot];
      self.lastShotFireTime = currentTime;
  }
```

This will call the -shoot method to launch a photon torpedo only after the difference between the last fire time and now is greater than the value in the shipFireRate property.

Now that we've added the ability to adjust the firing rate on the fly, we'll add the probability that a power-up will be dropped onto the scene by tweaking the -dropThing method so that we call the -dropPowerup every so often.

02-Actions/step07/SpaceRun/RCWMyScene.m
```
- (void)dropThing {
      u_int32_t dice = arc4random_uniform(100);

➤     if (dice < 5) {
➤         [self dropPowerup];
➤     } else if (dice < 20) {
          [self dropEnemyShip];
      } else {
          [self dropAsteroid];
      }
  }
```

This change means that a power-up will appear 5 percent of the time, an enemy ship 15 percent of the time, and an asteroid 80 percent of the time. Each of these probabilities is cumulative, which is why we first check to see whether the dice variable is less than five, followed by an else clause for less than twenty.

Now, we'll implement the power-up dropping method to create the node at a random starting point and travel down the screen.

02-Actions/step07/SpaceRun/RCWMyScene.m

```
- (void)dropPowerup
{
    CGFloat sideSize = 30;
    CGFloat startX = arc4random_uniform(self.size.width-60) + 30;
    CGFloat startY = self.size.height + sideSize;
    CGFloat endY = 0 - sideSize;

    SKSpriteNode *powerup = [SKSpriteNode spriteNodeWithImageNamed:@"powerup"];
    powerup.name = @"powerup";
    powerup.size = CGSizeMake(sideSize, sideSize);
    powerup.position = CGPointMake(startX, startY);
    [self addChild:powerup];

    SKAction *move = [SKAction moveTo:CGPointMake(startX, endY) duration:6];
    SKAction *spin = [SKAction rotateByAngle:-1 duration:1];
    SKAction *remove = [SKAction removeFromParent];

    SKAction *spinForever = [SKAction repeatActionForever:spin];
    SKAction *travelAndRemove = [SKAction sequence:@[move, remove]];
    SKAction *all = [SKAction group:@[spinForever, travelAndRemove]];
    [powerup runAction:all];
}
```

Nothing surprising here. It's an SKSpriteNode instance spinning and moving in a straight line from the top to the bottom of the screen. We're naming all these nodes "powerup" so we can find them at the top of the -checkCollisions method.

02-Actions/step07/SpaceRun/RCWMyScene.m

```
- (void)checkCollisions
{
    SKNode *ship = [self childNodeWithName:@"ship"];

➤   [self
➤    enumerateChildNodesWithName:@"powerup"
➤    usingBlock:^(SKNode *powerup, BOOL *stop) {
➤        if ([ship intersectsNode:powerup]) {
➤            [powerup removeFromParent];
➤            self.shipFireRate = 0.1;
➤        }
➤    }];
    // ...
}
```

Just like we did with the obstacles, if the ship bumps into a power-up, we remove it from the scene. Then we set the shipFireRate property to 0.1 photons a second. Now when the player collects these power-ups, the ship shoots faster!

Powering Down After a Few Seconds

The power-ups work, but they don't quite serve the game mechanics we're striving for. The ship needs to power down back to the normal shooting rate after five seconds. This is where Sprite Kit action blocks come in handy. Change the top of the -checkCollisions method to create an action sequence to restore the ship's fire rate.

```
02-Actions/step08/SpaceRun/RCWMyScene.m
- (void)checkCollisions
{
    SKNode *ship = [self childNodeWithName:@"ship"];
    [self
     enumerateChildNodesWithName:@"powerup"
     usingBlock:^(SKNode *powerup, BOOL *stop) {
        if ([ship intersectsNode:powerup]) {
            [powerup removeFromParent];
            self.shipFireRate = 0.1;

            SKAction *powerdown = [SKAction runBlock:^{
                self.shipFireRate = 0.5;
            }];
            SKAction *wait = [SKAction waitForDuration:5];
            SKAction *waitAndPowerdown = [SKAction sequence:@[wait, powerdown]];
            [ship runAction:waitAndPowerdown];
        }
    }];
    // ...
}
```

We use a -runBlock: action to create an Objective-C block of code that can run whatever we want. In this case, we set the shipFireRate property back to 0.5 seconds. We make a -waitForDuration: action and combine the two with a sequence action to delay that code by five seconds. Finally, we run it on the ship node itself, and boom—we've got temporary power-ups!

Well, we *almost* have the temporary power-ups we are trying to achieve. What happens if our ship touches another power-up before the previous one runs out? The way it's written now, the first power-down action block will run and restore the ship fire rate too soon, even though the player collected another one and we queued up another power-down action.

Instead, we want to stop the previous countdown and add a new one. That's where action keys come in. Sprite Kit lets us run actions with a key we can use to identify and remove them before they've had a chance to run. Let's use that by giving our power-down action the key waitAndPowerdown.

02-Actions/step09/SpaceRun/RCWMyScene.m

```
- (void)checkCollisions
{
    SKNode *ship = [self childNodeWithName:@"ship"];

    [self
     enumerateChildNodesWithName:@"powerup"
     usingBlock:^(SKNode *powerup, BOOL *stop) {
        if ([ship intersectsNode:powerup]) {
            [powerup removeFromParent];
            self.shipFireRate = 0.1;

            SKAction *powerdown = [SKAction runBlock:^{
                self.shipFireRate = 0.5;
            }];
            SKAction *wait = [SKAction waitForDuration:5];
            SKAction *waitAndPowerdown = [SKAction sequence:@[wait, powerdown]];
            [ship removeActionForKey:@"waitAndPowerdown"];
            [ship runAction:waitAndPowerdown withKey:@"waitAndPowerdown"];
        }
    }];
    // ...
}
```

We first call -removeActionForKey: to remove any existing power-down action that
might be there under that key. Nothing happens if there isn't already an
action with that key. Then we call -runAction:withKey: to apply the action and give
it the key as an identifier so we can remove it if the player collects another
power-up.

The net result is that collecting power-ups resets any countdown back to five
seconds and gives the player a strong incentive to find power-ups on the
screen whenever they show up. For the win!

You've finished diving deep into a very important piece of the Sprite Kit toolbox.
Actions let you manipulate nodes on the screen over time and free you up
from managing the size, shape, and other properties on your own. You can
mix and match simple actions to create marvelously complex behaviors,
identify them with keys, and apply them as granularly or as broadly as you
see fit. Sprite Kit actions are a very powerful tool! Check out Apple's documentation for a complete list.[5]

This game is quite playable now, but there are still some simple frills we can
add to make it more exciting. Next up, we're going to build explosions and
fire with the amazing Sprite Kit particle emitters.

---

5. https://developer.apple.com/library/ios/documentation/SpriteKit/Reference/SKAction_Ref/Reference/Reference.html

CHAPTER 3

Explosions and Particle Effects

Our game is developing nicely. We have single-finger game control, projectiles, enemies to avoid, and power-ups to collect. But a game's mechanics aren't the only things that make it fun. Many 2D games today add flair and polish in the form of particle effects. We, too, can give players a delightful experience with these special effects to catch their eye and stimulate their palate.

Sprite Kit makes it easy to implement many kinds of particle effects. We'll explore two different techniques based on the kind of feel we want to evoke in our game. You're going to learn the basics of particle emitting by rolling your own parallax star-field background that gives the illusion of zooming quickly through space. Once you understand how particle emitting works, we'll start using Apple's specialized SKEmitterNode to implement the ship thrusters and explosions.

Ready? Let's go!

Generating a Parallax Field of Stars

If we put this game in players' hands today, they'd think the ship was just sitting still while the dangerous asteroids and enemy ships flew past. But the ship is actually zooming ahead at full speed, trying to reach the destination. We need some sort of visual effect to evoke this feeling, and a fast-moving parallax star field will do the trick nicely.

We will implement this by creating our own *particle system*, which means that we'll generate and move nodes representing particles around on the screen based on a set of rules. For this effect, our particles are stars, and the rules are that they should travel from the top of the screen to the bottom, some faster than others to give the illusion of depth.

For simplicity, we will implement this particle system as a completely self-contained node that we add to our scene underneath all the other nodes. Let's call it RCWStarField. We'll create a new Objective-C class interface file named RCWStarField.h with these simple contents:

03-Particles/step01/SpaceRun/RCWStarField.h

```
#import <SpriteKit/SpriteKit.h>

@interface RCWStarField : SKNode
@end
```

We don't need to expose any methods on this SKNode subclass because it will be completely self-contained and run automatically when added to the scene.

Next, we'll create an Objective-C class implementation file named RCWStarField.m with this initialization method:

03-Particles/step01/SpaceRun/RCWStarField.m

```
#import "RCWStarField.h"
@implementation RCWStarField
- (instancetype)init
{
    if (self = [super init]) {
        __weak RCWStarField *weakSelf = self;
        SKAction *update =[SKAction runBlock:^{
            if (arc4random_uniform(10) < 3) {
                [weakSelf launchStar];
            }
        }];
        SKAction *delay = [SKAction waitForDuration:0.01];
        SKAction *updateLoop = [SKAction sequence:@[delay, update]];
        [self runAction:[SKAction repeatActionForever:updateLoop]];
    }
    return self;
}
@end
```

In the initializer, we are creating and running an action sequence that will repeat every tenth of a second for as long as the node is in the scene. Unlike SKScene objects that have an -update: method that is called by Sprite Kit on every frame, SKNode objects don't have that luxury. We could add a publicly visible -update: method and call it explicitly from the scene, but that defeats the purpose of having a self-contained particle system. Using our own private update loop will work better.

Note that because we need to call a method on self from inside the block, we must to create a weak reference to it. This is what we're doing with the weakSelf variable. The action holds a strong reference to the block, and the node holds a strong reference to the action. If the block held a strong reference to self (the node in this case), then the action, the block, and the node would form a retain cycle and never get deallocated. This weak-self setup is Apple's way of protecting against that cycle and stopping memory leaks. For a good refresher on retain cycles and blocks, check out Apple's documentation.[1]

Now, every time this update action is run, we throw the dice and execute the -launchStar method only 30 percent of the time. Let's implement that method next.

03-Particles/step01/SpaceRun/RCWStarField.m
```
- (void)launchStar
{
    CGFloat randX = arc4random_uniform(self.scene.size.width);
    CGFloat maxY = self.scene.size.height;
    CGPoint randomStart = CGPointMake(randX, maxY);

    SKSpriteNode *star = [SKSpriteNode spriteNodeWithImageNamed:@"shootingstar"];
    star.position = randomStart;
    star.size = CGSizeMake(2, 10);
    star.alpha = 0.1 + (arc4random_uniform(10) / 10.0f);
    [self addChild:star];

    CGFloat destY = 0 - self.scene.size.height - star.size.height;
    CGFloat duration = 0.1 + arc4random_uniform(10) / 10.0f;
    SKAction *move = [SKAction moveByX:0 y:destY duration:duration];
    SKAction *remove = [SKAction removeFromParent];
    [star runAction:[SKAction sequence:@[move, remove]]];
}
```

We're calculating a random starting point at the top of the screen and traveling to the bottom, just like we did when we sent the asteroids and power-ups on their path. Once a node is a child of the scene, the node can either walk up the parent nodes all the way to the scene object itself or simply use the scene property, as we're doing here, to get the scene's size for the calculations. This makes our star field reusable anywhere, and it will adjust to a scene's dimensions automatically.

We're creating an SKSpriteNode for the star with the shootingstar image texture, but we don't have that in our project yet. Drag the file shootingstar.png into the Xcode project sidebar and make sure you copy the file into the project directory, as in Figure 7, *Dragging and dropping files into the Xcode project*, on page 14. Note how we're randomly adjusting the size of the node and setting

---

1. https://developer.apple.com/library/ios/documentation/cocoa/conceptual/ProgrammingWithObjectiveC/Working-withBlocks/WorkingwithBlocks.html#//apple_ref/doc/uid/TP40011210-CH8-SW16

a random alpha to vary the transparency. For the alpha, we want to guarantee that the star isn't invisible, so we're adding 0.1 to make sure it shows up. Little tweaks like this help add to the effect of deep space. Feel free to play with the values to adjust to taste.

At the end of the method, we create the move-and-remove action sequence that makes the star travel down the screen and leave the scene when done. By using a random duration value for the move action, we get stars with different speeds. This gives the illusion of parallax, where things that are closer appear to pass by more quickly than things that are farther away, as you can see in the following figure.

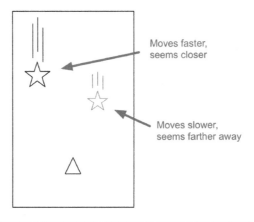

Figure 13—The parallax star effect

Our star-field particle system is complete! All we have to do now is add it to our scene. At the top of the RCWMyScene.m file, we'll import the interface.

03-Particles/step01/SpaceRun/RCWMyScene.m

```
#import "RCWStarField.h"
```

Then we'll create the node and add it to the scene at the very top of the -initWithSize: method.

03-Particles/step01/SpaceRun/RCWMyScene.m

```
- (id)initWithSize:(CGSize)size
{
    if (self = [super initWithSize:size]) {
        self.backgroundColor = [SKColor blackColor];

        RCWStarField *starField = [RCWStarField node];
        [self addChild:starField];
        // ...
```

That's it! No, really, it is! Our RCWStarField node is a self-contained particle system with its own update loop. As soon as we add it to the scene, the loop begins and the stars start flying. Because the stars remove themselves when they reach the bottom of the screen, there's nothing else we need to do.

This is the basic idea behind a particle emitter. It's a node representing a particle system that you add to a scene for a certain effect. Our emitter is a star field with specific rules for moving stars in a parallax fashion.

Rolling your own particle emitters is a great way to have fine-grained control over how the particles behave. But for many kinds of effects, such as explosions and fire, we don't have to roll our own. In fact, Sprite Kit comes with a visual editor to make up almost any kind of particle-spraying effect you can imagine! Let's dive into that next.

Building Thruster Fire with Xcode's Particle Editor

We're going to walk through how to use the Sprite Kit particle editor that comes with Xcode to add some exciting thruster fire to our valiant spaceship. First, choose File > New > File in Xcode. In the template picker, make sure iOS Resource is selected in the sidebar, select SpriteKit Particle File, and click Next, as shown in the following figure.

Figure 14—Creating a new particle file

When asked to choose a particle template, use the default Spark and click Next. Then name the file thrust.sks. You'll notice that the thrust.sks file and an accompanying spark.png texture file are now in the Xcode sidebar. Select thrust.sks in Xcode, and you'll see a flurry of activity in the live particle editor, as in the following figure.

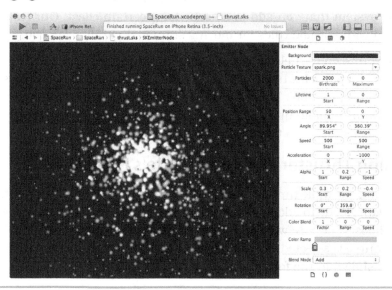

Figure 15—Xcode's new particle editor

On the left side, we see the particle emitter animation exactly as it will appear when added to our scene. On the right, we see a panel with all sorts of settings (Figure 16, *The thrust particle emitter settings*, on page 43). In fact, we are editing an instance of SKEmitterNode, and all these parameters line up with the properties on that node class. Feel free to browse that class's documentation to understand how they work. Here, we're going to aim for a particular kind of effect, and together we'll walk through the parameter settings to achieve it.

Notice how small the effect is, with a very slight trail out the bottom. We'll add this effect to the bottom of our ship node, which will give the appearance of a continuously firing thruster. Here's how each of the parameters works together:

- *Particle Texture*—This is set by the template you picked when creating the file. You don't have to use the default spark.png; you can substitute any image you want for the particles, but what comes out of the box will work fine for us.

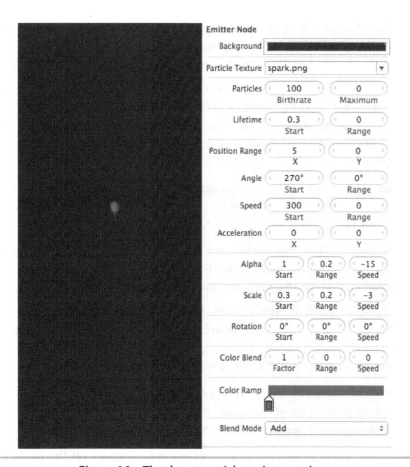

Figure 16—The thrust particle emitter settings

- *Particles*—We don't need a lot of nodes to achieve the small rocket-thrust effect, so a birthrate of 100 particles per second is fast enough. We're setting the maximum particle count to zero because the emitter stops once it reaches the set limit. We don't want it to stop yet. We'll control when the emitter stops in the game code itself.

- *Lifetime*—This controls how long the particles will live on the scene. In the star field we built, the lifetime of the particle was determined by how long it took to move to the bottom of the screen. Here, we're setting the starting lifetime to 0.3 seconds, after which the particles are removed. We can optionally set a range to control random variation of this value. That would make some particles appear to live longer than others, but it won't really matter here because of the tightly packed nature of this effect.

- *Position Range*—This controls the random starting distance from the emitter center for any new particle. By setting x to 5 and y to 0, we'll have a tightly confined birthplace that only varies horizontally a little bit.

- *Angle*—This controls the direction that the particles start to travel after they are born. Just like with the lifetime controls, you can specify a range to make it look like the collection of particles fans out, but in this case we want them flowing straight down, so we'll set the angle to 270 and the range to 0.

- *Speed*—This controls the starting speed of the particle, along with a random range. For our purposes, 300 is fast enough to stream away from the birthplace but not too fast to spread out. It makes for a tight flickering effect.

- *Acceleration*—Once the sprites are in motion, their speed can be affected by this acceleration vector. We'll make use of these when we get to explosions, but for the moment we'll set them to zero.

- *Alpha*—This controls the transparency of the particle over time. We're saying that the particles must start at fully opaque with an alpha of 1, give or take a 0.2 range. By using a speed of –15, we're making them disappear rapidly, again adding to the tightly packed effect.

- *Scale*—This does the same kind of manipulation as alpha but on the xScale and yScale properties of the node. We want the nodes to shrink away and disappear quickly, giving the effect of an efficient and clean burn.

- *Rotation*—This parameter has the effect you'd expect on the particle texture, but since the spark.png image is round, the rotation parameters don't matter for us. We're setting them to zero.

- *Color Blend*—This works together with the following *Color Ramp* and *Blend Mode* parameters to change the color of the particle over time. The color is set to red, and the rest of the parameters are left at the default values because we're changing the scale and alpha parameters to achieve the effect we want.

Those are the basics of the particle editor. It's easy to get lost fiddling with it to get it just right. This powerful particle system gives you the raw materials for all sorts of special effects. Our settings give us the specific effect we want —a tightly confined and flickering thrust effect that will add to the illusion of a thrilling space chase.

Now that we have this particle emitter, how do we add it to our ship? Let's look into loading emitter files.

Loading Particle Emitter Files

Unfortunately, loading particle emitter files into memory isn't as straightforward as loading sound files into actions, as we saw in *Playing Sound Effects in the Scene*, on page 28. For the moment, the Sprite Kit API doesn't give us a single method call to load and cache the file for later reuse. But that doesn't mean we can't implement it ourselves!

The *.sks files are archived SKEmitterNode instances. When we manipulate what we see in the Xcode particle editor, we're actually manipulating the real properties on this kind of node. When Xcode writes the particle emitter to disk, it uses the NSKeyedArchiver mechanism.

We can retrieve a copy of that node by loading it from the app bundle. To mimic the similar API that Apple uses for sound actions, we're going to build an Objective-C category to add a new method onto the SKEmitterNode class.[2] Create a new file in Xcode named SKEmitterNode+RCWExtensions.h with the following contents:

03-Particles/step02/SpaceRun/SKEmitterNode+RCWExtensions.h

```
#import <SpriteKit/SpriteKit.h>

@interface SKEmitterNode (RCWExtensions)

+ (SKEmitterNode *)rcw_nodeWithFile:(NSString *)filename;

@end
```

It's conventional to name object category files this way with the name of the extended class, a + symbol, and then the custom category name to describe what we're doing. In our category interface, we're naming the method rcw_nodeWithFile: with the rcw_ prefix because that's Apple's recommended way of ensuring that we don't clash with existing method names or other categories also extending this class.

It also makes it easy to search for in our code if Apple ever does implement this functionality in Sprite Kit and we want to deprecate or remove our method and use the official one.

Next, we'll create a file named SKEmitterNode+RCWExtensions.m with this initial implementation:

---

2. http://developer.apple.com/library/ios/documentation/cocoa/conceptual/ProgrammingWithObjectiveC/CustomizingExistingClasses/CustomizingExistingClasses.html

03-Particles/step02/SpaceRun/SKEmitterNode+RCWExtensions.m

```
#import "SKEmitterNode+RCWExtensions.h"

@implementation SKEmitterNode (RCWExtensions)

+ (SKEmitterNode *)rcw_nodeWithFile:(NSString *)filename
{
    NSString *basename = [filename stringByDeletingPathExtension];
    NSString *extension = [filename pathExtension];
    if ([extension length] == 0) {
        extension = @"sks";
    }
    NSString *path = [[NSBundle mainBundle] pathForResource:basename ofType:@"sks"];
    SKEmitterNode *node = (id)[NSKeyedUnarchiver unarchiveObjectWithFile:path];
    return node;
}

@end
```

We first check the file base name and extension, setting the extension to sks if there isn't one there. Apple's other class methods to load files permit you to leave off the extension if you want, so we should do that here, too. Then we grab the main bundle, ask it to give us the string path for a resource with the given name and file extension, and use the NSKeyedUnarchiver class to extract the SKEmitterNode. We're casting the result from the NSKeyedUnarchiver to id to tell the compiler not to complain, because it is expecting to return a more general NSObject.

Now, let's use this method to load our thrust effect and add it to the ship. In the RCWMyScene.m file, we'll add this line to import the category interface:

03-Particles/step02/SpaceRun/RCWMyScene.m

```
#import "SKEmitterNode+RCWExtensions.h"
```

And then, we'll add these lines to the -initWithSize: method after we add the ship to the scene:

03-Particles/step02/SpaceRun/RCWMyScene.m

```
- (id)initWithSize:(CGSize)size
{
    if (self = [super initWithSize:size]) {
        // ...
        [self addChild:ship];

➤       SKEmitterNode *thrust = [SKEmitterNode rcw_nodeWithFile:@"thrust.sks"];
➤       thrust.position = CGPointMake(0, -20);
➤       [ship addChild:thrust];
        //...
```

We're calling the -rcw_nodeWithFile: we just wrote on SKEmitterNode to get an instance of our thrust effect. We're setting the position using coordinates based on the ship node's own coordinate space and then adding it to the ship node. Remember from our discussion back in Chapter 1, *Introduction to Sprite Kit*, on page 1, that the nodes make up a tree. Children nodes act as part of their parent. By adding the thrust emitter node as a child of the ship at {0,-20}, the particle effect appears to be coming out of the back of the ship image as we see in the following figure.

Figure 17—The thrust emitter node as a child of the ship node

That's all it takes to add prefabricated SKEmitterNode particle effects to your game!

We're almost finished with particle systems for this level. Let's add the explosions next.

Spewing Particles Briefly for Explosions

We want to add explosions to the two collisions in our game: when the ship either shoots or collides with an obstacle. We'll build these particle emitters the same way we built the thrust emitter. Adding them to the scene is easy, but we have a problem. We don't want these emitters to keep running indefinitely. How do we make them die out and remove them from the scene after a short duration?

We use Sprite Kit actions, of course! Specifically, we'll use an action sequence to pause for a short duration, and then set the particle birthrate property to zero and wait for all the particles to die before removing the node. Because this is such a common operation for our emitters in this game and we already have a category to extend SKEmitterNode, let's add a new method that does this for us.

03-Particles/step03/SpaceRun/SKEmitterNode+RCWExtensions.m

```
- (void)rcw_dieOutInDuration:(NSTimeInterval)duration
{
    SKAction *firstWait = [SKAction waitForDuration:duration];
    __weak SKEmitterNode *weakSelf = self;
    SKAction *stop = [SKAction runBlock:^{
        weakSelf.particleBirthRate = 0;
    }];
    SKAction *secondWait = [SKAction waitForDuration:self.particleLifetime];
    SKAction *remove = [SKAction removeFromParent];
    SKAction *dieOut = [SKAction sequence:@[firstWait, stop, secondWait, remove]];
    [self runAction:dieOut];
}
```

We have two waiting periods because once we set the birthrate to zero, we still need to wait before the particles die out. Otherwise, the particles will vanish from the screen immediately, which isn't the effect we're looking for.

We need to add this method to the SKEmitterNode+RCWExtensions.h file so that our scene can call it:

03-Particles/step03/SpaceRun/SKEmitterNode+RCWExtensions.h

```
@interface SKEmitterNode (RCWExtensions)

+ (SKEmitterNode *)rcw_nodeWithFile:(NSString *)filename;
➤ - (void)rcw_dieOutInDuration:(NSTimeInterval)duration;

@end
```

Now we need to create the collision explosions. Create new particle emitter files named obstacleExplode.sks and shipExplode.sks and set the parameters to look like Figure 18, *The obstacle and ship explosion emitter settings*, on page 49.

Take some time to play with both of the .sks files in the 03-Particles/step03 project to note the differences and similarities. We're using the same spark.png particle texture. Because these are explosions, we're making the particles spread out in all directions, and we're giving the particles a slight downward acceleration to add to the illusion that we're zooming through space.

When a photon torpedo strikes and destroys an obstacle, the explosion should disperse and die out quickly because it will happen a lot during the game, and we don't want to obscure the player's vision. By contrast, when an obstacle strikes the ship, the explosion is slower and takes longer for the particles to shrink and fade away. Because that signals the end of the player's time in this round, we're taking our time to give it a majestic feel. Think of it like a moment of pause for the player to regroup and try again.

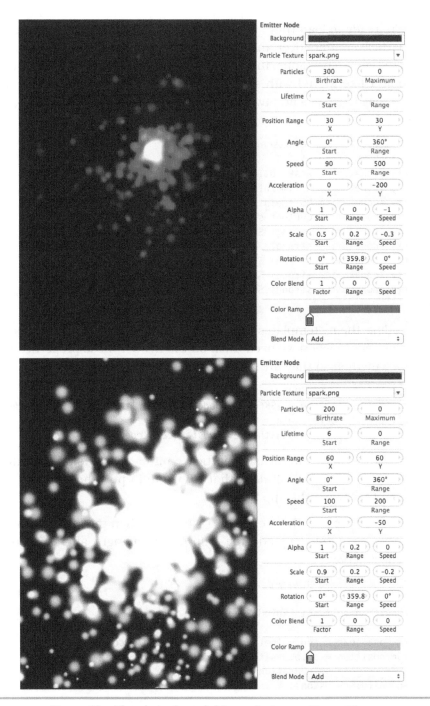

Figure 18—The obstacle and ship explosion emitter settings

Now we're ready to load these files into the game. Because we're going to be using particle emitters over and over, we don't want to load them from their files every time we need one. Instead, we will cache them in properties on the scene object like we did with sound actions in *Playing Sound Effects in the Scene*, on page 28. Let's add two properties for the emitter nodes in the class extension.

03-Particles/step03/SpaceRun/RCWMyScene.m
```
@interface RCWMyScene ()
@property (nonatomic, weak) UITouch *shipTouch;
@property (nonatomic) NSTimeInterval lastUpdateTime;
@property (nonatomic) NSTimeInterval lastShotFireTime;
@property (nonatomic) CGFloat shipFireRate;
@property (nonatomic, strong) SKAction *shootSound;
@property (nonatomic, strong) SKAction *shipExplodeSound;
@property (nonatomic, strong) SKAction *obstacleExplodeSound;
➤ @property (nonatomic, strong) SKEmitterNode *shipExplodeTemplate;
➤ @property (nonatomic, strong) SKEmitterNode *obstacleExplodeTemplate;
@end
```

We're calling them "templates" because we're going to use these nodes to make more nodes when we need them on the fly. Set these properties in the -initWithSize: method so they are ready when the scene is initialized.

03-Particles/step03/SpaceRun/RCWMyScene.m
```
self.shipExplodeTemplate = [SKEmitterNode rcw_nodeWithFile:@"shipExplode.sks"];
self.obstacleExplodeTemplate =
    [SKEmitterNode rcw_nodeWithFile:@"obstacleExplode.sks"];
```

Just like we did with the thruster particle emitter, we're using the category extension method on SKEmitterNode that we wrote to pull the data out of the particle emitter file in the app bundle.

Now we're ready to play these effects on the scene when the collisions happen in -checkCollisions. First, let's add the ship explosion right after running the sound-effect action.

03-Particles/step03/SpaceRun/RCWMyScene.m
```
// ...
[self runAction:self.shipExplodeSound];

➤ SKEmitterNode *explosion = [self.shipExplodeTemplate copy];
➤ explosion.position = ship.position;
➤ [explosion rcw_dieOutInDuration:0.3];
➤ [self addChild:explosion];
```

Notice how we're calling -copy on the node in the shipExplodeTemplate property. Nodes can only be added to a scene once. If we try to add a node again that already exists in the scene, then the game will crash with an error message.

We must add copies of particle emitter nodes, and we're using the emitter node in our cached properties as templates from which to make these copies.

Once we have our emitter-node copy, we set the position to where the obstacle was, tell it to start fading away after a tenth of a second with -rcw_dieOutInDuration:, and then add it to the scene. Let's do the same thing for the obstacle collisions.

```
03-Particles/step03/SpaceRun/RCWMyScene.m
[self runAction:self.obstacleExplodeSound];

➤ SKEmitterNode *explosion = [self.obstacleExplodeTemplate copy];
➤ explosion.position = obstacle.position;
➤ [explosion rcw_dieOutInDuration:0.1];
➤ [self addChild:explosion];

  *stop = YES;
```

Build and run the game. Houston, we have explosions!

And that's it for particle emitters. You started out learning how they work by creating your own emitter for stars in your deep-space star-field effect. Then we used the canned SKEmitterNode instances, courtesy of Xcode's particle editor, to complete the illusion of thrust and collisions.

If it's this simple to use the visual editor to create and load these particle systems, then why go to the trouble of building our own particle emitter for the star field? It all comes down to the rules that you want the particles to follow. SKEmitterNode instances are better for random and controlled spraying effects. Our star field had different needs that were more straightforward to achieve in custom code.

Still, SKEmitterNode objects offer a serious performance advantage. Drawing nodes on the screen doesn't come for free; the more nodes there are to manage, the more work Sprite Kit has to do, and the bigger potential for a drop in frame rate. SKEmitterNodes are fine tuned in a way that we can't achieve ourselves with the SKNode subclasses available to us. The particles are represented by private lightweight nodes that are very fast and let you run dense particle effects before you'll notice a slowdown on a device.

You'll make these kinds of tradeoffs quite often in game development. Try something to see whether it works. If you need more performance, try swtiching strategies.

This level of our game functions and looks great. Now let's figure out how to get the player into and out of the game with menus and cutscenes.

CHAPTER 4

Menus and Cutscenes

Most games don't just dive into the action. Often, they start at a menu of some kind that lets you fiddle with settings, or connect and review details on social game services, such as Game Center. Our game needs to let the player choose a difficulty level, so we'll need a menu, too. Also, many games have *cutscenes* that aren't part of the actual gameplay but show the backstory or build up tension with new details between levels. We need a chance to tell the story of our game, too, so we'll add an opening scene that scrolls the narrative past the player's eyes and out into space.

Sprite Kit has a lot of what we need but is still a relatively new technology. Building a menu with buttons and navigation can be quite complicated with just SKScene and SKNode objects. It would be nice if we could use bits and pieces of UIKit, Apple's standard iOS application development framework, which has solved a lot of these problems already. Things like UIButton, UISegmentedControl, UINavigationController, and gesture recognizers would come in handy.

Well, we're in luck! Sprite Kit and UIKit *can* play together in quite useful ways. This will give us a chance to explore how to use both to achieve our goals. Apple already gives us an interface editor for UIKit. Why not use it when it makes sense? We'll start by building a menu in the iOS application Storyboards. Then we'll learn about how Sprite Kit transitions work to build an opening scene introducing the player to the narrative of the game. Finally, we'll use a custom node to show the "Game Over" message and tell the player how to continue. By the end of this chapter, you'll have all the tricks you need to guide players in and out as they immerse themselves in your game.

Ready? Let's go!

Crafting a Basic Menu with UIKit's Interface Builder

For our first task, we're going to build a simple menu that lets the player choose either Easy or Hard mode. This mode setting will determine how often the obstacles appear on the screen. We'll provide a Play button that will transition the player immediately into the game. And as soon as the ship is destroyed, we'll send the player back out to the menu.

Up to this point we've been engrossed in Sprite Kit. It's a powerful and self-contained engine in its own right. But we don't have to abandon Apple's time-tested UIKit, especially with useful tools such as Interface Builder to help with layout and navigation. While we could build controls in Sprite Kit by laying out nodes and manually checking for touches, we'd be reinventing the wheel. For the purposes of this simple game, we can make excellent use of UIKit and get Sprite Kit to play along with it.

Sprite Kit runs entirely inside a special SKView object. It's a subclass of UIView, which means we can mix and match it at the bottom of a view hierarchy any way we want. In fact, we're already doing that. The storyboard that came with the Sprite Kit app template sets up an SKView instance as the view of the root view controller. We first noticed this back in Chapter 1, *Introduction to Sprite Kit*, on page 1, but ignored it up to this point. Now is the time to learn how it all works!

Customizing the Storyboard

Storyboards are Apple's way of letting the app developer build user interfaces and navigation flows in iOS applications. You use the Interface Builder tool as part of Xcode to set up view controllers and wire up the segues between them in response to different events.

This isn't a book about Storyboards, so we're going to gloss over a lot of things and assume you are starting with the baseline from the sample project that comes with the book. If you need a good refresher on Storyboards, check out the excellent book by Daniel Steinberg—*iOS Storyboards: An Animated Tour for iPhone and iPad Developers [Ste14]*—or Apple's documentation.[1]

If you've been building the app yourself as you follow along, you'll want to copy the Main.storyboard file from the 04-Menus/step01/SpaceRun/Base.lproj directory into your project, replacing what is there. We'll start with this file and walk through wiring up the outlets and actions in Interface Builder together.

Open the Main.storyboard file, and you'll see a layout like the following figure.

---

1. https://developer.apple.com/library/ios/referencelibrary/GettingStarted/RoadMapiOS/SecondTutorial.html

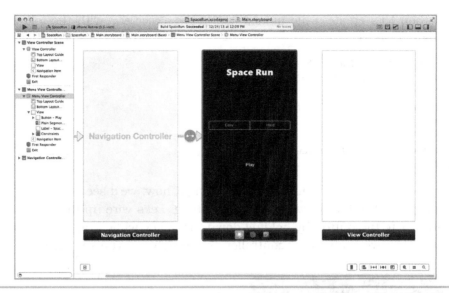

Figure 19—Storyboard for *Space Run*

The navigation controller is set up with a root view controller acting as our menu to get the player into the game. I've added the game title, a segmented control to choose game difficulty, and a button for transitioning to the original view controller that came with the Sprite Kit template—the view controller owning our game's SKView instance.

All the layout, colors, and font styling you see were set directly in Interface Builder using the sidebar inspectors. At the moment, Apple doesn't provide tools to visually manipulate Sprite Kit objects, other than the particle editor we met back in Chapter 3, *Explosions and Particle Effects*, on page 37. It's obvious that Apple will improve the state of Sprite Kit tools, but for now Storyboards will serve us well as a design tool and will let us use the best of what UIKit has to offer.

We're ready to write the supporting code behind this interface. The storyboard is expecting the root view controller to be an instance of RCWMenuViewController, which doesn't exist yet. In the project, let's create a new file named RCWMenuViewController.h with these contents:

04-Menus/step01/SpaceRun/RCWMenuViewController.h

```
#import <UIKit/UIKit.h>

@interface RCWMenuViewController : UIViewController

@end
```

And then let's create a file named RCWMenuViewController.m with the following contents to start:

04-Menus/step01/SpaceRun/RCWMenuViewController.m
```
#import "RCWMenuViewController.h"

@interface RCWMenuViewController ()
@end

@implementation RCWMenuViewController
@end
```

If we were to build and launch the game right now, we'd see our menu, but tapping the Play button wouldn't do anything. Let's wire up the game view controller to the button by holding down the ^ key while dragging from the Play button over to the view controller on the right, as you see here:

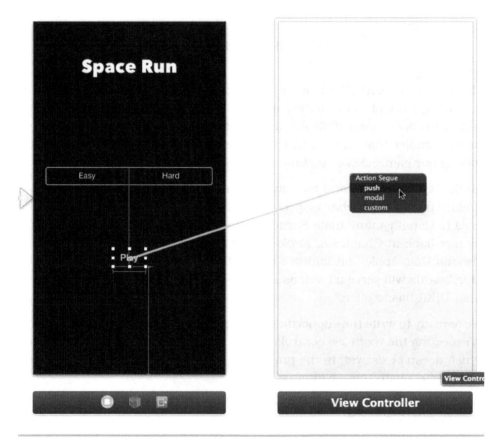

Figure 20—Wiring up the Play button

Choose Push from the pop-up menu after you release the mouse button. You've now wired up a segue to push the game view controller on the stack when the button is tapped. Run the game, and you'll see the nifty new menu. Tap the button, and the game will start, just as we expect.

Returning to the Menu When the Game Is Over

Everything works great to get us *into* the game, but alas the game doesn't bring us back to the menu when the ship explodes and the game is over. Let's work on that next.

Popping the navigation controller stack once we know the game has ended is the easy part. But how do we communicate to the game view controller that the game is over? In our code, the RCWMyScene class knows the state of the game and knows when our game ends. Let's create a public property in the header file for an Objective-C block that we'll invoke when the ship explodes. In RCWMyScene.h, let's add the following line:

```
04-Menus/step02/SpaceRun/RCWMyScene.h
@interface RCWMyScene : SKScene
@property (nonatomic, copy) dispatch_block_t endGameCallback;
@end
```

With the endGameCallback property declared, we need to call it at the right time. In RCWMyScene.m, we'll change the part of the -checkCollisions method where we check for a ship intersecting with an obstacle and add this line:

```
04-Menus/step02/SpaceRun/RCWMyScene.m
[self
 enumerateChildNodesWithName:@"obstacle"
 usingBlock:^(SKNode *obstacle, BOOL *stop) {
    if ([ship intersectsNode:obstacle]) {
        self.shipTouch = nil;
        // ...
        [self endGame];
    }
    // ...
```

We'll use this -endGame method as the place to do all the cleanup when the ship is destroyed. Right now, we just need to invoke the endGameCallback block.

```
04-Menus/step02/SpaceRun/RCWMyScene.m
- (void)endGame
{
    NSAssert(self.endGameCallback, @"Forgot to set the endGameCallback");
    self.endGameCallback();
}
```

We have to check to see whether the endGameCallback property is set before we call it. All properties are nil by default. Sending messages to nil objects is fine because of the way the Objective-C message passing works, but trying to invoke a nil block will cause a memory access error and crash the game with a vague and unhelpful error message. Using an NSAssert() like this will ensure that the app fails with a more helpful error message if we try to end the game without setting this property.

Then, in the RCWViewController class that is responsible for setting up the Sprite Kit view for our game, we need to set the endGameCallback property so we can pop the navigation stack. Let's change the -viewDidLoad method in RCWViewController.m to look like this:

```
04-Menus/step02/SpaceRun/RCWViewController.m
- (void)viewDidLoad
{
    [super viewDidLoad];

    SKView *skView = (SKView *)self.view;
    skView.showsFPS = YES;
    skView.showsNodeCount = YES;

➤   RCWMyScene *scene = [RCWMyScene sceneWithSize:skView.bounds.size];
    scene.scaleMode = SKSceneScaleModeAspectFill;

➤   __weak RCWViewController *weakSelf = self;
➤   scene.endGameCallback = ^{
➤       [weakSelf.navigationController popViewControllerAnimated:YES];
➤   };

    [skView presentScene:scene];
}
```

There's a lot more going on here in this code block than we're ready to discuss yet. The -viewDidLoad method was generated for us by the Sprite Kit template back in Chapter 1, *Introduction to Sprite Kit*, on page 1. We'll talk more about the details behind setting up the SKView object in *Showing the Star Field Underneath UIKit*, on page 62. For now, just note the highlighted section where we set the endGameCallback property to a block that calls -popViewControllerAnimated: on the navigation controller. Also note that we're playing it safe and using a weak reference to self inside the block. For a refresher about why we need to do that, refer back to *Generating a Parallax Field of Stars*, on page 37.

And that's it! Since our view controller pops the navigation stack when the endGameCallback block is invoked, the player will return to the main menu when the game ends. Alas, this isn't quite what we want yet, because the player doesn't get a chance to see the ship explosion. It's abrupt, but we've solved the current problem of ending the game and returning to the main menu. We'll tackle the end-game sequence soon in *Building a Game-Ending Sequence*, on page 72.

Setting Up Player Difficulty

We want the player's difficulty level choice in the menu to affect the game, so we need to figure out how to communicate the value of the difficulty control down to our game scene. UISegmentedControl lives in RCWMenuViewController's view. Our SKMyScene scene lives in the original RCWViewController that came with the Sprite Kit template. How do we get the choice from the segmented control down to our game code?

We pass it along, of course! First, let's give ourselves access to the control itself. We'll create a property in RCWMenuViewController.h as an outlet for the storyboard.

```
04-Menus/step03/SpaceRun/RCWMenuViewController.m
@interface RCWMenuViewController ()
➤ @property (nonatomic, strong) IBOutlet UISegmentedControl *difficultyChooser;
@end
```

Now let's go to the Storyboards file, select the menu view controller, and then in the left scene browser sidebar, ^-drag from the Menu View Controller to the segmented control and choose the difficultyChooser property outlet that we just created, as shown:

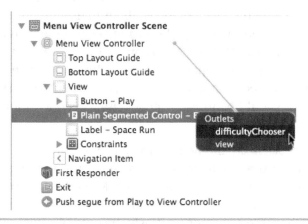

Figure 21—Wiring up the difficulty control

The menu view controller doesn't have a reference to the game scene, so we have to pass the choice the player made to the game's view controller first.

Then we'll be able to pass that down into our game scene. In the RCWViewController.h file, let's add this property definition:

04-Menus/step03/SpaceRun/RCWViewController.h

```
@interface RCWViewController : UIViewController
➤ @property (nonatomic) BOOL easyMode;
@end
```

Because our game has only two modes, Easy and Hard, we're using a Boolean value to keep track of whether we're supposed to be in Easy mode.

Back in RCWMenuViewController.m, import the RCWViewController.h header file.

04-Menus/step03/SpaceRun/RCWMenuViewController.m

```
#import "RCWViewController.h"
```

Then we'll implement the -prepareForSegue:sender: method.

04-Menus/step03/SpaceRun/RCWMenuViewController.m

```
- (void)prepareForSegue:(UIStoryboardSegue *)segue sender:(id)sender
{
    if ([segue.identifier isEqualToString:@"PlayGame"]) {
        RCWViewController *gameController = segue.destinationViewController;
        gameController.easyMode = self.difficultyChooser.selectedSegmentIndex == 0;
    } else {
        NSAssert(false, @"Unknown segue identifier %@", segue.identifier);
    }
}
```

The -prepareForSegue:sender: method is Apple's way of letting us do important work as a storyboard segues between view controllers. Each segue can have an identifier to distinguish which one is about to execute. In this case, we're checking for the name matching the string "PlayGame", and if we have a match then we grab the RCWViewController out of the destinationViewController property and set the easyMode property based on the value of the difficultyChooser control. If the selected segment index is zero, then the first segment is selected, and we should be in Easy mode. Otherwise, we should be in Hard mode.

If this -prepareForSegue:sender: method doesn't recognize the segue identifier, then we should assume that we mistyped something into the storyboard. That's why we're throwing an assertion error with NSAssert(). It causes the app to crash and burn with a useful error message in the log to figure out what went wrong, rather than silently ignoring it, which could be a difficult bug to find.

Of course, this means we need to name the segue that begins the game. In the storyboard, click on the segue between the menu and gameplay view controllers. In the right storyboard sidebar, choose the Attributes Inspector icon and set the identifier to PlayGame, as shown:

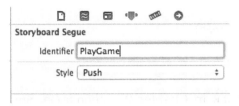

We're almost finished wiring up the difficulty chooser. We've set the easyMode property on the game's view controller, but we still need to pass that value down into the scene. Let's create the same easyMode property in the RCWMyScene.h header file.

```
04-Menus/step03/SpaceRun/RCWMyScene.h
@interface RCWMyScene : SKScene
@property (nonatomic, copy) dispatch_block_t endGameCallback;
➤ @property (nonatomic) BOOL easyMode;
@end
```

And then in the RCWViewController.m file, we'll set the scene's easyMode property to the controller's easyMode property in the -viewDidLoad method.

```
04-Menus/step03/SpaceRun/RCWViewController.m
// ...
➤ scene.easyMode = self.easyMode;

    __weak RCWViewController *weakSelf = self;
    scene.endGameCallback = ^{
        [weakSelf.navigationController popViewControllerAnimated:YES];
    };
// ...
```

Our scene now has the correct easyMode value. All that's left is to change our game logic to react appropriately. In the -update: method of the RCWMyScene.m file, we'll change how we call the -dropThing method to pick a probability.

```
04-Menus/step03/SpaceRun/RCWMyScene.m
- (void)update:(NSTimeInterval)currentTime
{
    // ...

➤     NSInteger thingProbability;
➤     if (self.easyMode) {
➤         thingProbability = 15;
➤     } else {
➤         thingProbability = 30;
➤     }
➤
```

```
➤    if (arc4random_uniform(1000) <= thingProbability) {
➤        [self dropThing];
➤    }

    [self checkCollisions];

    self.lastUpdateTime = currentTime;
}
```

As we discussed back in Chapter 2, *Actions: Go, Sprite, Go!*, on page 13, increasing the frequency that obstacles and power-ups drop onto the scene is a good way to increase the difficulty.

Phew! That was a lot of work, but it's the standard way of passing information from one view controller to the next with Storyboards. Run the game and enjoy the two difficulty levels. See how far you get in the Hard mode!

Storyboards are the way to visually build and design navigation flows in iOS. There's no reason we can't use them for our Sprite Kit games, too. Because we're using standard UIKit controls, we have all their power available to us to customize them using the storyboard inspectors and the UIAppearance protocols.

We've built a simple menu and difficulty chooser for our game to give players some control over their experience. Next, you're going to learn how to do some more fancy integration with UIKit by embedding Sprite Kit animations *underneath* your UIKit controls!

Showing the Star Field Underneath UIKit

Our menu is done, but it's bland. It would be nice if we could play some animations from our game underneath the menu, like our star field. Well, with Sprite Kit, we can!

All of the Sprite Kit magic in an SKScene object gets rendered in a special UIView subclass called an SKView. Because it's a member of the view hierarchy, we can put an SKView anywhere we want on any iOS interface. Note that normal controls and views cannot interact directly with Sprite Kit nodes because nodes exist entirely within the Sprite Kit world. Also, Sprite Kit views are always opaque, so you can't overlay nodes on top of a standard user interface. But still, this gives us a lot of power to use Sprite Kit for visualizations underneath UIKit.

Let's use this to our advantage by inserting an SKView instance with a scene that displays our star field. First, we'll begin by importing the RCWStarField.h header file and adding a new property to the RCWMenuViewController.m class extension.

04-Menus/step04/SpaceRun/RCWMenuViewController.m
```
#import "RCWMenuViewController.h"
#import "RCWViewController.h"
```
➤ ```
#import "RCWStarField.h"
```

```
@interface RCWMenuViewController ()
@property (nonatomic, strong) IBOutlet UISegmentedControl *difficultyChooser;
```
➤ ```
@property (nonatomic, strong) SKView *demoView;
@end
```

Next, we'll build up an SKView and its corresponding scene in the -viewDidAppear:
method of the RCWMenuViewController. There's no need to subclass; we can just
create the objects we need on the fly.

04-Menus/step04/SpaceRun/RCWMenuViewController.m
```
- (void)viewDidAppear:(BOOL)animated
{
    [super viewDidAppear:animated];

    self.demoView = [[SKView alloc] initWithFrame:self.view.bounds];

    SKScene *scene = [[SKScene alloc] initWithSize:self.view.bounds.size];

    scene.backgroundColor = [SKColor blackColor];
    scene.scaleMode = SKSceneScaleModeAspectFill;

    SKNode *starField = [RCWStarField node];
    [scene addChild:starField];

    [self.demoView presentScene:scene];

    [self.view insertSubview:self.demoView atIndex:0];
}
```

In this method we first create a new SKView instance that is the same size as
the view controller's view bounds. Then we create a plain vanilla SKScene with
a black background color and aspect fill scale mode. The scale mode doesn't
matter for our game because it's meant to be played in portrait orientation.
We're just using the same scale mode that Apple supplied for us in the template. If your game allows players to rotate their device to a different orientation
while playing, or if you want to scale up an iPhone game to a larger iPad
screen, then you might want to investigate the different modes to fit your
needs.

We then create an instance of the RCWStarField node and add it to the scene.
Remember that we created this node back in Chapter 3, *Explosions and Particle Effects*, on page 37, and because it's a self-contained SKNode subclass,
we can reuse it here easily.

Finally, we tell the SKView subclass we're holding in the demoView property to present the scene, which tells the Sprite Kit world to start doing its magic. We add that demo view to the *bottom* of the view hierarchy by telling the view controller's view to -insertSubview:atIndex: with an index of zero.

Before we can try this out, we need to clean up after ourselves in the -viewDidDisappear: method.

04-Menus/step04/SpaceRun/RCWMenuViewController.m
```
- (void)viewDidDisappear:(BOOL)animated
{
    [super viewDidDisappear:animated];

    [self.demoView removeFromSuperview];
    self.demoView = nil;
}
```

By removing the demo view when the view controller is no longer visible and releasing it, we're getting rid of the Sprite Kit rendering context so it doesn't take up precious CPU cycles or battery power. It will be re-created when the view controller is presented after the game ends anyway.

Run the game, and you'll see the magic of the fast-moving parallax star field behind the UIKit controls!

The fact that Sprite Kit's views are just a UIView subclass means that we have tremendous power to use Sprite Kit as background glitter for anything. You can even use this to display animations and demonstrations in plain old iOS applications. It's not just for games! Remember the limitations, though. Sprite Kit nodes don't interact with anything outside their scene or the SKView. The SKView objects are always opaque. If you want UIKit to talk to things living in Sprite Kit (and vice versa), you'll have to provide the conduit and pass messages around yourself.

Next up, you will learn about Sprite Kit scene transitions to make a cutscene that tells the origin story behind the game!

Custom Scenes and Gesture Recognizers

A common way to tell the backstory of a game to players is with a cutscene —a pause in the gameplay to prepare players for the next task. Some games use videos or very complex productions to get the point across. For our streamlined game, we're going to use a separate SKScene with scrolling text to tell players why their ship is traveling at breakneck speeds through space. Here's the effect we're going for. You might recognize it from an obscure 1970s sci-fi movie.

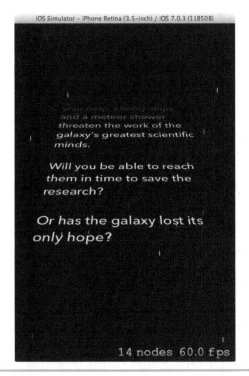

Figure 22—The opening *Star Wars*–style text crawl

To implement this, you'll need to learn a lot more about how SKScene objects work and how to control their containing SKView object on the fly. We'll implement the paragraphs of text with a UITextView and use a UITapGestureRecognizer object to let us know if the player taps to skip the cutscene and jump straight into the game.

Let's start by writing a special SKScene class for our opening scene. Create an RCWOpeningScene.h interface header file with these contents:

```
04-Menus/step05/SpaceRun/RCWOpeningScene.h
#import <SpriteKit/SpriteKit.h>

@interface RCWOpeningScene : SKScene
@property (nonatomic, copy) dispatch_block_t sceneEndCallback;
@end
```

We're adding a sceneEndCallback block property because we need some way for this scene to communicate to the outside world that the opening scene animation is finished. The object that is responsible for transitioning to the next scene will provide the block.

Next, we'll begin the class implementation in a new file named RCWOpeningScene.m.

04-Menus/step05/SpaceRun/RCWOpeningScene.m
```
#import "RCWOpeningScene.h"
#import "RCWStarField.h"

@implementation RCWOpeningScene

- (void)didMoveToView:(SKView *)view
{
    self.backgroundColor = [SKColor blackColor];

    RCWStarField *starField = [RCWStarField node];
    [self addChild:starField];
}
```

The first order of business is to set the background color to black and then add the star-field node. We're getting a lot of mileage out of this node, both here and in the demo view under our menu. Keep this in mind as you structure your own games. Break common things out into nodes so you can reuse them.

When presenting SKScene objects in an SKView, this -didMoveToView: method gets called, similar to the view controller lifecycle methods like -viewDidAppear: and the others. We know for certain that by the time this method is called, our scene has settled within an SKView, and we can do whatever special initialization we need. Yes, we could have set up the star field in the -initWithSize: method like we do in the RCWMyScene object, but we'll keep all the initialization code together here for simplicity.

Next, we want to create the slow, slanted text-crawl effect. Let's define two view properties in the class definition of RCWOpeningScene above the implementation.

04-Menus/step05/SpaceRun/RCWOpeningScene.m
```
@interface RCWOpeningScene ()
@property (nonatomic, strong) UIView *slantedView;
@property (nonatomic, strong) UITextView *textView;
@end
```

Why are we using UIKit views here? While Sprite Kit provides special text-label nodes (which we'll get to use soon), it doesn't support line-wrapping paragraphs of text. Also, Core Animation makes it absurdly simple to transform UIView objects in the three-dimensional way we want. Basically, using these two view properties and UIKit is the easiest way to pull off the effect we're going for.

At the end of the -didMoveToView: method, let's add this nice chunk of verbose Objective-C:

04-Menus/step05/SpaceRun/RCWOpeningScene.m
```
// ...
// Create a superview that will do the perspective tilt.
self.slantedView = [[UIView alloc] initWithFrame:self.view.bounds];
self.slantedView.opaque = NO;
self.slantedView.backgroundColor = [UIColor clearColor];
[self.view addSubview:self.slantedView];

// Tilt the superview
CATransform3D transform = CATransform3DIdentity;
transform.m34 = -1.0 / 500.0;
transform = CATransform3DRotate(transform, 45.0f * M_PI / 180.0f, 1.0f,
                                0.0f, 0.0f);
[self.slantedView.layer setTransform:transform];
```

We start by creating a superview slanted with a 3D transform to give it depth. Again, this is a book focusing specifically on Sprite Kit, so we're only briefly mentioning what's going on here. If you're new to iOS development and want some more backstory on UIKit and Core Animation, remember to check out the book *iOS SDK Development [AD12]*.

Next, we create a text view with the right styles and text of our backstory positioned below the visible region of the superview.

04-Menus/step05/SpaceRun/RCWOpeningScene.m
```
// ...
// Use a textview to display our back story
self.textView = [[UITextView alloc] initWithFrame:
                CGRectInset(self.view.bounds, 30, 0)];
self.textView.opaque = NO;
self.textView.backgroundColor = [UIColor clearColor];
self.textView.textColor = [UIColor yellowColor];
self.textView.font = [UIFont fontWithName:@"AvenirNext-Medium" size:20];

self.textView.text = @"A distress call comes in from thousands of light "
                     "years away. The colony is in jeopardy and needs "
                     "your help. Enemy ships and a meteor shower "
                     "threaten the work of the galaxy's greatest "
                     "scientific minds.\n\n"
                     "Will you be able to reach "
                     "them in time to save the research?\n\n"
                     "Or has the galaxy lost it's only hope?";
self.textView.userInteractionEnabled = NO;
self.textView.center = CGPointMake(self.size.width / 2 + 15,
                                   self.size.height + (self.size.height / 2));
[self.slantedView addSubview:self.textView];
```

Next we add a special gradient layer mask on top to make up the fadeaway effect as the text scrolls upward and out into space.

04-Menus/step05/SpaceRun/RCWOpeningScene.m

```
// ...
// Add a fading mask so it vanishes out of sight
CAGradientLayer *gradient = [CAGradientLayer layer];
gradient.frame = view.bounds;
gradient.colors = @[(id)[[UIColor clearColor] CGColor],
                    (id)[[UIColor whiteColor] CGColor]];
gradient.startPoint = CGPointMake(0.5, 0.0);
gradient.endPoint = CGPointMake(0.5, 0.20);
[self.slantedView.layer setMask:gradient];
```

Last, we run the animation over the span of twenty seconds to move the text view slowly upward in the coordinate space of the slanted view.

04-Menus/step05/SpaceRun/RCWOpeningScene.m

```
// ...
[UIView
 animateWithDuration:20
 delay:0
 options:UIViewAnimationOptionCurveLinear
 animations:^{
     self.textView.center = CGPointMake(self.size.width / 2,
                                        0 - (self.size.height / 2));
 } completion:^(BOOL finished) {
     NSAssert(self.sceneEndCallback, @"Scene end callback not set.");
     self.sceneEndCallback();
 }];
```

This will create a linear animation that will appear to send the text view out into space because of the 3D transformation on its superview. After the animation completes, we invoke the sceneEndCallback block using the same NSAssert() check we used before to make sure a block is set.

Because we are manipulating the SKView from within this scene, we'll want to put that view back the way it was when the scene is done. That's why we should implement the -willMoveFromView: method as follows.

04-Menus/step05/SpaceRun/RCWOpeningScene.m

```
- (void)willMoveFromView:(SKView *)view
{
    [self.slantedView removeFromSuperview];
    self.slantedView = nil;
    self.textView = nil;
}
```

We remove the slanted subview from the SKView and set both properties to nil to release them. The SKView is now pristine and ready to complete the transition to the next SKScene object.

Phew! That's a lot of code to get our effect. Alas, that's the price of quality animation. At least it's all self-contained here in this class. All we have to do is present this scene in our SKView instance.

Let's rearrange our game's view controller to control how the opening scene appears. First, we'll import the opening scene file at the top of RCWViewController.m.

04-Menus/step05/SpaceRun/RCWViewController.m

```
#import "RCWViewController.h"
#import "RCWMyScene.h"
➤ #import "RCWOpeningScene.h"
```

Then, we'll change the -viewDidLoad method to present a blank scene with a black background.

04-Menus/step05/SpaceRun/RCWViewController.m

```
- (void)viewDidLoad
{
    [super viewDidLoad];

    SKView *skView = (SKView *)self.view;
    skView.showsFPS = YES;
    skView.showsNodeCount = YES;

➤    SKScene *blackScene = [[SKScene alloc] initWithSize:skView.bounds.size];
➤    blackScene.backgroundColor = [SKColor blackColor];
➤    [skView presentScene:blackScene];
}
```

By starting with this black scene, we can fade in the opening scene as we transition to it in the -viewDidAppear: method.

04-Menus/step05/SpaceRun/RCWViewController.m

```
- (void)viewDidAppear:(BOOL)animated
{
    [super viewDidAppear:animated];

    SKView *skView = (SKView *)self.view;

    RCWOpeningScene *scene = [RCWOpeningScene sceneWithSize:skView.bounds.size];
    scene.scaleMode = SKSceneScaleModeAspectFill;
    SKTransition *transition = [SKTransition fadeWithDuration:1];
    [skView presentScene:scene transition:transition];

    // ...
```

As soon as the view appears, we create the RCWOpeningScene instance and transition to it by passing an SKTransition effect to the -presentScene:transition: method on SKView. You can use all kinds of slick (and sometimes cheesy) transition effects. Read up on the SKTransition class documentation for more info.

Once the scene is presented, we need to set the sceneEndCallback property to a block that does the original work to start the game.

04-Menus/step05/SpaceRun/RCWViewController.m

```
    // ...
    __weak RCWViewController *weakSelf = self;
    scene.sceneEndCallback = ^{
        RCWMyScene *scene = [RCWMyScene sceneWithSize:skView.bounds.size];
        scene.scaleMode = SKSceneScaleModeAspectFill;
        scene.easyMode = weakSelf.easyMode;
        scene.endGameCallback = ^{
            [weakSelf.navigationController popViewControllerAnimated:YES];
        };
        SKTransition *transition = [SKTransition fadeWithColor:[SKColor blackColor]
                                                      duration:1];
        [skView presentScene:scene transition:transition];
    };
}
```

Inside the block, we create our RCWMyScene game class that we've been using all along, set the easyMode property and endGameCallback like before, and then transition to it by fading through black.

It's finally ready to test! Give it a whirl. Build and run the game. When you tap the Play button, you'll see the opening scene animation. After the text finishes crawling over twenty seconds, the scenes will transition and the game will start.

Using Gesture Recognizers from Within a Scene

We can't quite check this game off as completed, though. At the moment, every time players start a new game, they have to wait for the full twenty seconds of opening animation to complete. It would be nice to let users skip it if they want to by, say, tapping anywhere on the screen.

A tap gesture recognizer would be perfect for this use case, but we can't apply gesture recognizers to scenes or nodes. Gesture recognizers only work with UIView subclasses, but because we can access the SKView from within the scene, we can add and remove the recognizer on the fly!

First, we need a property to keep track of the gesture recognizer. We'll add the following line to the class extension at the top of the file.

04-Menus/step06/SpaceRun/RCWOpeningScene.m

```
@interface RCWOpeningScene ()
@property (nonatomic, strong) UIView *slantedView;
@property (nonatomic, strong) UITextView *textView;
➤ @property (nonatomic, strong) UITapGestureRecognizer *tapGesture;
@end
```

Next, at the very end of the -didMoveToView: method, we'll create a tap gesture recognizer for the SKView and have it call a method on our scene.

04-Menus/step06/SpaceRun/RCWOpeningScene.m
```
// ...
self.tapGesture = [[UITapGestureRecognizer alloc]
                      initWithTarget:self action:@selector(endScene)];
[self.view addGestureRecognizer:self.tapGesture];
```

This will call the -endScene method on this class as soon as a tap is detected. We'll move all the work to end the scene into this method in a moment.

We need to undo our alterations to the SKView and remove the gesture recognizer in the -willMoveFromView: method.

04-Menus/step06/SpaceRun/RCWOpeningScene.m
```
- (void)willMoveFromView:(SKView *)view
{
➤    [self.view removeGestureRecognizer:self.tapGesture];
➤    self.tapGesture = nil;

     [self.slantedView removeFromSuperview];
     self.slantedView = nil;
     self.textView = nil;
}
```

And we need to change the completion block to call the -endScene method as well.

04-Menus/step06/SpaceRun/RCWOpeningScene.m
```
[UIView
 animateWithDuration:20
 delay:0
 options:UIViewAnimationOptionCurveLinear
 animations:^{
     self.textView.center = CGPointMake(self.size.width / 2,
                                        0 - (self.size.height / 2));
 } completion:^(BOOL finished) {
➤    if (finished) {
➤        [self endScene];
➤    }
 }];
```

Notice that we're first checking to see whether the finished flag passed into the completion block is true. We need to do this because we will be canceling this scrolling animation if we detect a tap early. A canceled animation will pass in a NO to our block, and if that's the case, then we already know that we've triggered the end of the scene. We'll just leave the completion block without doing anything else.

Now, let's write the -endScene method.

04-Menus/step06/SpaceRun/RCWOpeningScene.m

```
- (void)endScene
{
    [UIView animateWithDuration:0.3 animations:^{
        self.textView.alpha = 0;
    } completion:^(BOOL finished) {
        [self.textView.layer removeAllAnimations];
        NSAssert(self.sceneEndCallback, @"Scene end callback not set.");
        self.sceneEndCallback();
    }];
}
```

Even though our SKScene object will transition with a fade to the game scene, the textView that we added to the SKView won't fade away automatically. We need to fade it away first. After it vanishes, we're removing all animations that could still be running on the textView's layer. This will stop the scrolling if need be and call that animation's completion block with NO so we don't trigger this -endScene method again.

Finally, we call the sceneEndCallback, which tells the view controller to present the game scene, and the game begins.

As you can see, using gesture recognizers with Sprite Kit isn't quite as straightforward as with the standard UIKit components. Sprite Kit is optimized for low-level touch handling. But we are still able to use gesture recognizers to some degree by manipulating a scene's SKView when the scene is presented and when it leaves.

Those are the basics of building custom scenes and using gesture recognizers. We've got our narrative cutscene to prepare players before they dive into the game. Now we just need to give them a consoling pat on the back when the game ends!

Building a Game-Ending Sequence

Remember when we first implemented the -endGame method on our game's RCWMyScene class? As soon as the ship explodes, we immediately transition back to the menu. That's too abrupt. Instead, let's show a consoling "Game Over" on the screen as the explosion particle emitter dies out and the obstacles continue falling.

While we could build a whole new cutscene to display to the player, that would replace everything going on in the SKView. We're not going to present a new SKScene instance, because we want the activity that the player left behind on the game scene to continue behind the end-game message. Let's build a self-contained node that will display the "Game Over" text, animate it into place, and then display some instructions for the user to tap the screen to play again. We'll add this node to our game scene at the appropriate moment and make it wait for a tap to continue.

First, let's create a new header file named RCWGameOverNode.h with these contents:

04-Menus/step07/SpaceRun/RCWGameOverNode.h
```
#import <SpriteKit/SpriteKit.h>

@interface RCWGameOverNode : SKNode
@end
```

Next, we'll start the implementation of this node in a new file named RCWGameOverNode.m with this -init method:

04-Menus/step07/SpaceRun/RCWGameOverNode.m
```
#import "RCWGameOverNode.h"

@implementation RCWGameOverNode

- (instancetype)init
{
    if (self = [super init]) {
        SKLabelNode *label = [SKLabelNode
                                  labelNodeWithFontNamed:@"AvenirNext-Heavy"];
        label.fontSize = 32;
        label.fontColor = [SKColor whiteColor];
        label.text = @"Game Over";
        [self addChild:label];
    }
    return self;
}

@end
```

Here we are meeting the SKLabelNode for the first time. This special node displays text in whatever font we want.[2] Alas, the label nodes don't support line breaks or word wrapping, so we'd have to handle those things ourselves. That's why it was easier to use a UITextView for the paragraphs of text we slowly crawled across the screen in the opening animation. Still, for single lines of text that need to be shown among other nodes in a scene, SKLabelNode instances do just fine.

---

2.   View http://iosfonts.com for a list of font names that come bundled with iOS.

Next, let's animate this node by making it fade in and scale up to full size.

04-Menus/step07/SpaceRun/RCWGameOverNode.m
```
// ...
label.alpha = 0;
label.xScale = 0.2;
label.yScale = 0.2;

SKAction *fadeIn = [SKAction fadeAlphaTo:1 duration:2];
SKAction *scaleIn = [SKAction scaleTo:1 duration:2];
SKAction *fadeAndScale = [SKAction group:@[fadeIn, scaleIn]];
[label runAction:fadeAndScale];
```

We're setting the starting properties for alpha, xScale, and yScale and then using the familiar SKAction objects to run the animations.

Now we can add and animate the instructions for the user to tap the screen.

04-Menus/step07/SpaceRun/RCWGameOverNode.m
```
// ...
SKLabelNode *instructions = [SKLabelNode
                                labelNodeWithFontNamed:@"AvenirNext-Medium"];
instructions.fontSize = 14;
instructions.fontColor = [SKColor whiteColor];
instructions.text = @"Tap to try again.";
instructions.position = CGPointMake(0, -45);
[self addChild:instructions];

instructions.alpha = 0;
SKAction *wait = [SKAction waitForDuration:4];
SKAction *appear = [SKAction fadeAlphaTo:1 duration:0.2];
SKAction *popUp = [SKAction scaleTo:1.1 duration:0.1];
SKAction *dropDown = [SKAction scaleTo:1 duration:0.1];
SKAction *pauseAndAppear = [SKAction sequence:@[wait, appear, popUp, dropDown]];
[instructions runAction:pauseAndAppear];
```

Just like before, we create an SKLabelNode with the text to instruct the user, but this time we use an action to delay for a moment before showing it, for effect.

Our RCWGameOverNode is finished! It's a fully self-contained node. All we have to do is bring it into our RCWMyScene and display it at the right time.

At the top of the RCWMyScene.m file, we'll add the import statement for the RCWGameOverNode.h header file.

04-Menus/step07/SpaceRun/RCWMyScene.m
```
#import "RCWGameOverNode.h"
```

Because we want to listen for a tap gesture when the end of the game is reached, we'll add a property to the class extension to hold the gesture recognizer.

04-Menus/step07/SpaceRun/RCWMyScene.m

```
@interface RCWMyScene ()
@property (nonatomic, weak) UITouch *shipTouch;
@property (nonatomic) NSTimeInterval lastUpdateTime;
@property (nonatomic) NSTimeInterval lastShotFireTime;
@property (nonatomic) CGFloat shipFireRate;

@property (nonatomic, strong) SKAction *shootSound;
@property (nonatomic, strong) SKAction *shipExplodeSound;
@property (nonatomic, strong) SKAction *obstacleExplodeSound;

@property (nonatomic, strong) SKEmitterNode *shipExplodeTemplate;
@property (nonatomic, strong) SKEmitterNode *obstacleExplodeTemplate;

@property (nonatomic, strong) UITapGestureRecognizer *tapGesture;
@end
```

We'll replace the -endGame method to instead register the tap gesture recognizer and add our RCWGameOverNode to the scene.

04-Menus/step07/SpaceRun/RCWMyScene.m

```
- (void)endGame
{
    self.tapGesture = [[UITapGestureRecognizer alloc]
                          initWithTarget:self action:@selector(tapped)];
    [self.view addGestureRecognizer:self.tapGesture];
    RCWGameOverNode *node = [RCWGameOverNode node];
    node.position = CGPointMake(self.size.width / 2, self.size.height / 2);
    [self addChild:node];
}
```

Once this method is called, the recognizer will be immediately registered on the scene's view and will call the -tapped method to let us know the player is ready to continue. We don't need to do anything special when we add the RCWGameOverNode object to the scene. It will automatically run the animation actions.

Now, we'll implement the -tapped method to do what the -endGame method used to do.

04-Menus/step07/SpaceRun/RCWMyScene.m

```
- (void)tapped
{
    NSAssert(self.endGameCallback, @"Forgot to set the endGameCallback");
    self.endGameCallback();
}
```

We're checking the endGameCallback property and then invoking the block to signal that the player is finished with the game and we can return to the menu.

But we're not finished yet! Remember that adding a gesture recognizer to a scene's view needs to be undone when the scene is removed from the view. We'll add this -willMoveFromView: method at the end of the scene implementation.

04-Menus/step07/SpaceRun/RCWMyScene.m
```
- (void)willMoveFromView:(SKView *)view
{
    [self.view removeGestureRecognizer:self.tapGesture];
    self.tapGesture = nil;
}
```

Now we have a game-over sequence that plays when the ship explodes, and the game listens for the player's tap to return to the main menu. Go ahead, try out the game and see how it works!

We've explored a few different ways to build menus and cutscenes in our games. By leveraging the tried-and-true UIKit tools, we can use Storyboards to build up a navigation flow to let the player configure and enter the game. This gives us a lot of flexibility to lay out what we want. When we're ready for more fine-grained control within Sprite Kit, we can drop down to SKScene objects and handle labels, animations, transitions, and touches manually—whatever it takes to achieve the effects we want. The sky—even the galaxy—is the limit.

Figure 23—The end of the game

Up next, we'll complete this game by talking a bit about strategies for keeping track of a player's score and how to lay out nodes on the screen for a heads-up display.

CHAPTER 5

Keeping Score with a Heads-Up Display

Our *Space Run* game is quite fun to play, but we're missing an important element—bragging rights! We need to display the score during gameplay in a way that the player can glance at during the heat of the action. That's a great use case for a stationary *heads-up display* (HUD).

First conceived for aircraft pilots to have important status information displayed on a transparent window so they could keep their "heads up" during flight, a heads-up display is now a staple of game design. We're going to build a custom node that acts as this kind of stationary display within our game. This node will be responsible for laying out its children nodes within the scene. It will keep track of the score and the elapsed game time. We'll even throw in a visible countdown for power-ups and a high-score display on the main menu of the game at the end.

Ready? Let's go!

Planning the Node Layout

Before we get started in code, let's take a step back and imagine what we want to achieve. Otherwise, we could get lost trying to keep our brains organized as we calculate the position of everything we need to display. Figure 24, *Sketching out the heads-up display*, on page 78 shows a sketch representing what we're aiming for.

We're using two labels as "titles" to describe what we're displaying, and two labels as "values" underneath. We'll need to lay them out on the left and right sides of the screen and remember to use number formatters so we get all the standard goodies, such as the thousands separators and proper decimal rounding.

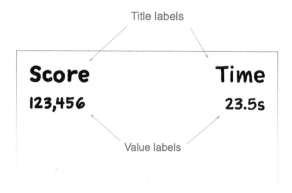

Figure 24—Sketching out the heads-up display

To help us lay all this out, we're going to create a special HUD node for our heads-up display that will hold everything. Once this node is added to the scene, we'll tell it to lay out its children nodes. But these children nodes won't be the labels. Instead, we'll use blank nodes as group containers and lay out the label nodes within them like in the following figure.

Figure 25—Breaking up the display into groups

These group nodes are not anything special, just simple SKNode objects with the label nodes as children. By themselves, plain SKNode objects don't display anything on the screen. But when they contain child nodes, they all behave like a unit. Change the position of one of these SKNode objects that we're using as a group, and everything inside moves along with it. This is the same mechanism we used to add the ship thruster particle emitter to the ship node back in *Building Thruster Fire with Xcode's Particle Editor*, on page 41. For a refresher on the node scene graph, review Figure 5, *Nodes laid out in a scene graph*, on page 5.

Organizing our label nodes into groups like this simplifies our layout. We'll left-align the score title and value labels and right-align the time title and value. These parent group nodes are then easily positioned on the left and right sides of the scene. Because the labels are properly aligned and anchored within their respective groups, there's nothing else we need to do. Even if the scene size were to differ—say, on an iPad—the code that moves the groups to the corners would just work.

Let's prepare the HUD node and add it to our scene so we'll be ready to start building this node hierarchy. We'll create a new file named RCWHUDNode.h in the Xcode project to define the interface for our HUD node like this:

```
05-HUD/step01/SpaceRun/RCWHUDNode.h
#import <SpriteKit/SpriteKit.h>

@interface RCWHUDNode : SKNode
@end
```

We'll fill in this interface as we realize what methods we'll need. Next, we'll create a new file named RCWHUDNode.m with an empty implementation.

```
05-HUD/step01/SpaceRun/RCWHUDNode.m
#import "RCWHUDNode.h"

@interface RCWHUDNode ()
@end

@implementation RCWHUDNode
@end
```

Now that we've created the RCWHUDNode class, we can use it in the RCWMyScene object. Let's import the header file at the top of the RCWMyScene.m file.

```
05-HUD/step01/SpaceRun/RCWMyScene.m
#import "RCWMyScene.h"
#import "RCWStarField.h"
#import "SKEmitterNode+RCWExtensions.h"
#import "RCWGameOverNode.h"
➤ #import "RCWHUDNode.h"
```

And then we'll initialize and add the RCWHUDNode as the last setup step in the -initWithSize: method.

```
05-HUD/step01/SpaceRun/RCWMyScene.m
RCWHUDNode *hudNode = [RCWHUDNode node];
hudNode.name = @"hud";
hudNode.zPosition = 100;
hudNode.position = CGPointMake(size.width/2, size.height/2);
[self addChild:hudNode];
```

We're creating the node and naming it so we can find it later. But this time, we're setting the zPosition property to some number greater than zero. By default, nodes overlap according to the order they were added to the scene. This HUD node is one of the first to be made a child, so if we don't set the zPosition property, it will appear to be beneath everything else added later. That's not what we want, because enemies and asteroids will cover it up as they are added to the scene and fly down. We're arbitrarily choosing 100 as the value here, but in practice you would use this property to make sure all the visual components are layered the way you expect in the scene. At this point, we just want to guarantee that our HUD is always on top.

We're also setting the position of the node to the dead center of the scene. This is important because all the child nodes of our HUD will be positioned relative to the node's origin at the center. Because we know the HUD node is at the center of the scene and we know the scene size, we can use this information to calculate where the labels need to appear in the top corners of the scene.

Running the game right now won't show anything new on the screen, but we've got the raw scaffolding in place so we can start experimenting with the design next.

Aligning Label Nodes Within Groups

To match the design of our HUD, we need two parent nodes as groups to hold the title and value labels for the score and the elapsed time. Let's start by building the first group, and you'll learn how to align text label nodes inside it. We'll create an empty node as the score group and then add the two label nodes as children. We'll add an -init method to the top of the implementation in RCWHUDNode.m.

```
05-HUD/step02/SpaceRun/RCWHUDNode.m
- (instancetype)init
{
    if (self = [super init]) {
        SKNode *scoreGroup = [SKNode node];
        scoreGroup.name = @"scoreGroup";
        SKLabelNode *scoreTitle =
            [SKLabelNode labelNodeWithFontNamed:@"AvenirNext-Medium"];
        scoreTitle.fontSize = 12;
```

```
    scoreTitle.fontColor = [SKColor whiteColor];
    scoreTitle.horizontalAlignmentMode = SKLabelHorizontalAlignmentModeLeft;
    scoreTitle.verticalAlignmentMode = SKLabelVerticalAlignmentModeBottom;
    scoreTitle.text = @"SCORE";
    scoreTitle.position = CGPointMake(0, 4);
    [scoreGroup addChild:scoreTitle];

    // ...
  }
  return self;
}
```

This initializer will be called when the RCWHUDNode is created. Inside, we build an empty SKNode as our first containing group and naming it scoreGroup so we can find it later when we lay it out in the scene. Then we create an SKLabelNode object for the scoreTitle with a font size and color that matches the look we are going for.

We set the vertical and horizontal alignment modes in such a way to help us lay out the two labels inside this group node. Because we want this score title to be on top, we are saying that it should be vertically aligned along the bottom of the text and four points above the origin. And because this title is on the left side of the scene, we are also left-justifying it horizontally.

To help visualize what's going on, take a look at the following figure.

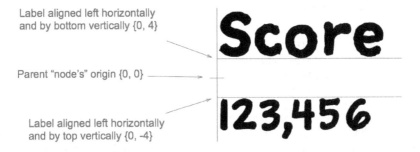

Figure 26—Aligning and laying out labels around the group origin

Remember that child nodes are positioned relative to the parent node's origin. By using bottom vertical alignment, left horizontal alignment, and positioning the title label at {0, 4}, we now have a parent node, scoreGroup, that we can position on the left side of the scene, and we know the labels will align the way we want.

We have the title label node, but we need to complete this group by adding the value label node.

05-HUD/step02/SpaceRun/RCWHUDNode.m
```
SKLabelNode *scoreValue =
    [SKLabelNode labelNodeWithFontNamed:@"AvenirNext-Bold"];
scoreValue.fontSize = 20;
scoreValue.fontColor = [SKColor whiteColor];
scoreValue.horizontalAlignmentMode = SKLabelHorizontalAlignmentModeLeft;
scoreValue.verticalAlignmentMode = SKLabelVerticalAlignmentModeTop;
scoreValue.name = @"scoreValue";
scoreValue.text = @"0";
scoreValue.position = CGPointMake(0, -4);
[scoreGroup addChild:scoreValue];
```

It's a very similar setup to the title label node we just created, but this time it is vertically aligned along the top. When this node is positioned at {0, -4}, that places it four points below the center of this scoreGroup node, and the net effect is that the alignment makes it look as if these two labels are flush left and separated by eight points vertically between them.

Next, we add the scoreGroup node to the RCWHUDNode.

05-HUD/step02/SpaceRun/RCWHUDNode.m
```
[self addChild:scoreGroup];
```

This RCWHUDNode is now a grandparent! It has a child node we are using as a container to group its child nodes that display the text for the score title and value. We need to do the same thing for the game elapsed time. Let's create the elapsedGroup node and the two label children.

05-HUD/step02/SpaceRun/RCWHUDNode.m
```
SKNode *elapsedGroup = [SKNode node];
elapsedGroup.name = @"elapsedGroup";
SKLabelNode *elapsedTitle =
    [SKLabelNode labelNodeWithFontNamed:@"AvenirNext-Medium"];
elapsedTitle.fontSize = 12;
elapsedTitle.fontColor = [SKColor whiteColor];
elapsedTitle.horizontalAlignmentMode = SKLabelHorizontalAlignmentModeRight;
elapsedTitle.verticalAlignmentMode = SKLabelVerticalAlignmentModeBottom;
elapsedTitle.text = @"TIME";
elapsedTitle.position = CGPointMake(0, 4);
[elapsedGroup addChild:elapsedTitle];
SKLabelNode *elapsedValue =
    [SKLabelNode labelNodeWithFontNamed:@"AvenirNext-Bold"];
elapsedValue.fontSize = 20;
elapsedValue.fontColor = [SKColor whiteColor];
elapsedValue.horizontalAlignmentMode = SKLabelHorizontalAlignmentModeRight;
elapsedValue.verticalAlignmentMode = SKLabelVerticalAlignmentModeTop;
elapsedValue.name = @"elapsedValue";
elapsedValue.text = @"0.0s";
elapsedValue.position = CGPointMake(0, -4);
[elapsedGroup addChild:elapsedValue];
```

We name this group node elapsedGroup so we can find it later and build the title and value label nodes just like we did for the score. Because this set of nodes will be on the right side of the screen, we're using SKLabelHorizontalAlignmentModeRight horizontal alignment mode to make sure they line up flush to the right —the mirror opposite of what we did for the score labels on the left.

Next, we'll add this elapsedGroup label to the RCWHUDNode.

05-HUD/step02/SpaceRun/RCWHUDNode.m

```
[self addChild:elapsedGroup];
```

At the moment, we have all the labels properly laid out within their respective parent nodes, but both of these group nodes are centered within the HUD by default. We want to trigger some sort of layout method so that these group nodes are properly positioned to the top left and right when this HUD is added to the scene.

SKNode instances don't know when they're added to a scene, so we need to build an explicit method on this RCWHUDNode object to do the layout work, and we'll call it at the right time. Let's call this method -layoutForScene. We'll put this line in the RCWHUDNode.h file to expose this method to anyone using this class.

05-HUD/step02/SpaceRun/RCWHUDNode.h

```
@interface RCWHUDNode : SKNode
➤ - (void)layoutForScene;
@end
```

And we'll write this method in the RCWHUDNode.m file to find our group nodes and position them in the top corners of the scene.

05-HUD/step02/SpaceRun/RCWHUDNode.m

```
- (void)layoutForScene
{
    NSAssert(self.scene, @"Cannot be called unless added to a scene");
    CGSize sceneSize = self.scene.size;
    CGSize groupSize = CGSizeZero;
    SKNode *scoreGroup = [self childNodeWithName:@"scoreGroup"];
    groupSize = [scoreGroup calculateAccumulatedFrame].size;
    scoreGroup.position = CGPointMake(0 - sceneSize.width/2 + 20,
                                      sceneSize.height/2 - groupSize.height);
    SKNode *elapsedGroup = [self childNodeWithName:@"elapsedGroup"];
    groupSize = [elapsedGroup calculateAccumulatedFrame].size;
    elapsedGroup.position = CGPointMake(sceneSize.width/2 - 20,
                                        sceneSize.height/2 - groupSize.height);
}
```

When a node exists in the scene graph, it can get access to the scene through its scene property. That property is nil if the node doesn't belong to a scene yet, and this method isn't very useful until the node is added to a scene. So we're using the NSAssert() macro to cause a fatal error if the self.scene property is nil. This will give us instant feedback while developing if we try to call this method without a scene. The game will crash with the given error message in the log.

Once we guarantee that this node is in a scene, we grab the scene's size and store it off in the sceneSize variable for use in our calculations. We also create a groupSize variable initialized to CGSizeZero that we'll reuse to help us calculate the precise position of each group.

We look up our scoreGroup node by its string name that we gave it when we created it. We call -calculateAccumulatedFrame on that group node to have it check all of its children and grandchildren and add up their frames to give us the enclosing frame around this node. That provides enough information to calculate how far down from the top of the scene this node should be.

Remember that child nodes are positioned relative to their parent node's origin. Because the RCWHUDNode will be at the center of the scene, we do all our calculations on these labels moving them to the left or the right of the center of this HUD node. That's why we set the scoreGroup.position property so the x-coordinate is 0 - sceneSize.width/2 + 20. That says that we want this score group node to be half the scene width to the left, and we add 20 points to nudge it back to the right to create a margin.

We also set the y-coordinate to sceneSize.height/2 - groupSize.height because we want it to be half the scene height up minus the full height of this score group.

Phew! I know that sounds like a lot of work, but it's the best way to lay out a lot of nodes within a scene. Building up our layout with smaller groups and then positioning those groups according to their size and the scene's size helps to make our layouts flexible and easy to adapt to different screen sizes and orientations.

All that's left to do is call this -layoutForScene method after it is added to the scene in the -initWithSize: method of the RCWMyScene.m file.

```
05-HUD/step02/SpaceRun/RCWMyScene.m
RCWHUDNode *hudNode = [RCWHUDNode node];
hudNode.name = @"hud";
hudNode.zPosition = 100;
hudNode.position = CGPointMake(size.width/2, size.height/2);
[self addChild:hudNode];
```

➤ [hudNode layoutForScene];

Our HUD is dynamically positioning its child nodes. So if we ever choose to build an iPad version, the HUD will lay out with the wider scene size without any problem at all. A good rule of thumb: Lay things out on paper first to get the feel for what should be grouped together and how they are aligned. Then lay out the groups. Build up your design piece by piece, and everything will fall into place.

Next, let's talk about updating this HUD during gameplay.

Updating the Display

The HUD is looking great on the screen, but it's not useful until we can update it with the proper information in real time. We need to be able to add points to the score, start some sort of timer that updates the display of elapsed time, and stop the timer when the game ends. We'll implement methods for each of these behaviors and call them at the appropriate time in the scene.

Let's declare these three behaviors as public methods in the RCWHUDNode.h header file.

```
05-HUD/step03/SpaceRun/RCWHUDNode.h
@interface RCWHUDNode : SKNode
- (void)layoutForScene;

➤ - (void)addPoints:(NSInteger)points;
➤ - (void)startGame;
➤ - (void)endGame;
➤
@end
```

These methods will let us command and control this node from the scene. Because this node will be accumulating the points for the score and keeping track of time, let's also expose two public properties in this interface so we can ask for this information later.

```
05-HUD/step03/SpaceRun/RCWHUDNode.h
@property (nonatomic) NSTimeInterval elapsedTime;
@property (nonatomic) NSInteger score;
```

Remember back in *Drawing Scenes and Sprite Nodes*, on page 3, when we discussed how nodes act as both the data model of the game and the mechanism for display? Well, we're seeing that play out here. This HUD node displays and serves as the final authority of the current score as well as the player's clock.

We're ready to start building the implementations of these methods in the RCWHUDNode.m file. We'll start by building the method that adds new points to the score.

05-HUD/step03/SpaceRun/RCWHUDNode.m

```
- (void)addPoints:(NSInteger)points
{
    self.score += points;

    SKLabelNode *scoreValue =
        (SKLabelNode *)[self childNodeWithName:@"scoreGroup/scoreValue"];
    scoreValue.text = [NSString stringWithFormat:@"%@",
                        [self.scoreFormatter stringFromNumber:@(self.score)]];

    SKAction *scale = [SKAction scaleTo:1.1 duration:0.02];
    SKAction *shrink = [SKAction scaleTo:1 duration:0.07];
    SKAction *all = [SKAction sequence:@[scale, shrink]];
    [scoreValue runAction:all];
}
```

We increment the score property to add in the new points. Then, we look up the scoreValue label node by its name using a special search syntax. Remember that the score value label is *not* a child node of RCWHUDNode. It's a child node of our scoreGroup node that we are using to group and lay out the score title and value labels. We can look up this grandchild node by using the "score-Group/scoreValue" search syntax. This says to first find the scoreGroup child within *this* node and then find the node named scoreValue as a child of *that* node. This way we don't have to keep references to subnodes. Finding grandchildren is as simple as using a name path.

Because we want the scores to be formatted with the thousands separator, we're using an NSNumberFormatter object that we'll cache in the self.scoreFormatter property. Let's define that property in the class extension at the top of RCWHUDNode.m.

05-HUD/step03/SpaceRun/RCWHUDNode.m

```
@property (nonatomic, strong) NSNumberFormatter *scoreFormatter;
```

And then at the end of the -init method, let's initialize the number formatter with decimal style.

05-HUD/step03/SpaceRun/RCWHUDNode.m

```
self.scoreFormatter = [[NSNumberFormatter alloc] init];
self.scoreFormatter.numberStyle = NSNumberFormatterDecimalStyle;
```

Formatting objects, such as what we use for dates and numbers, are expensive to create but cheap to use. They do a lot of internal setup to prepare themselves for the styles we request, and caching them like this is important—especially because we'll be formatting numbers quite often while updating the display.

Our score method is finished. Let's implement the method to start the game timer.

05-HUD/step03/SpaceRun/RCWHUDNode.m

```
- (void)startGame
{
    NSTimeInterval startTime = [NSDate timeIntervalSinceReferenceDate];
    SKLabelNode *elapsedValue =
        (SKLabelNode *)[self childNodeWithName:@"elapsedGroup/elapsedValue"];

    __weak RCWHUDNode *weakSelf = self;
    SKAction *update = [SKAction runBlock:^{
        NSTimeInterval now = [NSDate timeIntervalSinceReferenceDate];
        NSTimeInterval elapsed = now - startTime;
        weakSelf.elapsedTime = elapsed;
        elapsedValue.text = [NSString stringWithFormat:@"%@s",
                          [weakSelf.timeFormatter stringFromNumber:@(elapsed)]];
    }];

    SKAction *delay = [SKAction waitForDuration:0.05];
    SKAction *updateAndDelay = [SKAction sequence:@[update, delay]];
    SKAction *timer = [SKAction repeatActionForever:updateAndDelay];
    [self runAction:timer withKey:@"elapsedGameTimer"];
}
```

Remember back in *Generating a Parallax Field of Stars*, on page 37, when we needed a recurring update loop to build our star-field particle emitter? Well, we're using the same mechanism here to continually update our elapsed time label so players know how long they've been playing the game.

We first calculate the timestamp when we started the timer in the startTime variable. We look up the elapsedValue label using the same kind of grandchild search path we did for the score value label. Then we build a sequence of actions that make our clock tick. Every 0.05 seconds, we'll run a block that updates the elapsedTime property to be the difference between the startTime timestamp and the current timestamp.

Note that we're running this action with the key, elapsedGameTimer. We'll get back to that in a moment.

When we update the elapsed time value label, we want a number formatter that always displays the tenths decimal place, even if it is zero. Let's do the same thing we did for the scoreFormatter and set it up as a property.

05-HUD/step03/SpaceRun/RCWHUDNode.m

```
@property (nonatomic, strong) NSNumberFormatter *timeFormatter;
```

Then we'll initialize that number formatter at the end of the -init method.

```
05-HUD/step03/SpaceRun/RCWHUDNode.m
self.timeFormatter = [[NSNumberFormatter alloc] init];
self.timeFormatter.numberStyle = NSNumberFormatterDecimalStyle;
self.timeFormatter.minimumFractionDigits = 1;
self.timeFormatter.maximumFractionDigits = 1;
```

This number formatter uses the decimal style like our score formatter, but we're forcing it to always show the tenths decimal place by setting minimumFractionDigits and maximumFractionDigits to one.

With our -startGame method complete, we now turn our attention to the -endGame method, which will stop the timer.

```
05-HUD/step03/SpaceRun/RCWHUDNode.m
- (void)endGame
{
    [self removeActionForKey:@"elapsedGameTimer"];
}
```

That's all it takes. Remember that we ran the repeating sequence of actions with the key, elapsedGameTimer. To stop the timer sequence, we just need to remove the action for that key.

Our HUD behavior methods are complete. Let's use them in the scene! Back in RCWMyScene.m, at the end of the -initWithSize: method, add the call to tell the HUD node that the game has started.

```
05-HUD/step03/SpaceRun/RCWMyScene.m
  [hudNode layoutForScene];
➤ [hudNode startGame];
```

This tells the HUD node to create and run the timer action sequence that both calculates the elapsed time and updates the display.

We then need to tell the HUD node that the game is over in the scene's -endGame method.

```
05-HUD/step03/SpaceRun/RCWMyScene.m
  - (void)endGame
  {
      self.tapGesture = [[UITapGestureRecognizer alloc]
                            initWithTarget:self action:@selector(tapped)];
      [self.view addGestureRecognizer:self.tapGesture];

      RCWGameOverNode *node = [RCWGameOverNode node];
      node.position = CGPointMake(self.size.width / 2, self.size.height / 2);
      [self addChild:node];
➤     RCWHUDNode *hud = (RCWHUDNode *)[self childNodeWithName:@"hud"];
➤     [hud endGame];
  }
```

We look up the RCWHUDNode by name and tell it that the game has ended. This will remove the action that updates the elapsed time.

All that's left is to update the score. Scoring is a fascinating topic of game design that could take up many pages all by itself. For our purposes, we can keep it simple. To reward the player for staying alive, we're going to make the points the player earns for every destroyed obstacle increase as a multiple of the elapsed time. And we'll also double the points for each obstacle again if the game is played on Hard mode. More player effort brings more reward.

In the collision detection where a photon node intersects with an obstacle node, let's add these three lines to calculate and increase the score:

```
05-HUD/step03/SpaceRun/RCWMyScene.m
[self
 enumerateChildNodesWithName:@"photon"
 usingBlock:^(SKNode *photon, BOOL *stop) {
    if ([photon intersectsNode:obstacle]) {
        [photon removeFromParent];
        [obstacle removeFromParent];
        [self runAction:self.obstacleExplodeSound];
        SKEmitterNode *explosion = [self.obstacleExplodeTemplate copy];
        explosion.position = obstacle.position;
        [explosion rcw_dieOutInDuration:0.1];
        [self addChild:explosion];
➤       RCWHUDNode *hud = (RCWHUDNode *)[self childNodeWithName:@"hud"];
➤       NSInteger score = 10 * hud.elapsedTime * (self.easyMode ? 1 : 2);
➤       [hud addPoints:score];
        *stop = YES;
    }
}];
```

We find the RCWHUDNode in the scene by name, compute the score as a function of elapsed time and the difficulty level, and then tell the node to add those points to the score it already has.

Go ahead and play the game. Fun, eh? Let's add some extra panache next and show a countdown timer so players know how long they have left when the weapon is powered up.

Pulsing Power-Up Countdowns for the Win

At the moment, players have no idea how much time they have left when they collect a power-up to temporarily enhance their weapon. While the authors originally thought this was an important game mechanic, we realized when play testing this behavior that it was more frustrating for players than we'd like. Let's add more information to see whether it aids players' strategy and helps their sense of progress.

Because we already have a heads-up display, let's add a red, pulsing countdown timer that shows players how long until their current power-up runs out. The figure here shows what we're looking for.

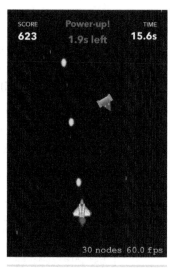

The hypothesis is that this gives players enough information to decide when to collect other power-ups they see on the screen, or avoid them altogether if they think they have enough time left and there is too much in the way.

Adding this to the game is easy because we've separated out the responsibility into the RCWHUDNode object.

First, we want to add a new method in the RCWHUDNode.h header so we can tell the node that the player collected a power-up.

Figure 27—Showing a power-up countdown in the center

```
05-HUD/step04/SpaceRun/RCWHUDNode.h
@interface RCWHUDNode : SKNode
- (void)layoutForScene;
- (void)addPoints:(NSInteger)points;
- (void)startGame;
- (void)endGame;
➤ - (void)showPowerupTimer:(NSTimeInterval)time;

@property (nonatomic) NSTimeInterval elapsedTime;
@property (nonatomic) NSInteger score;
@end
```

Now that we have a public interface for our scene to interact with, next we need a new group of nodes to hold the title and value labels for the power-up timer in the -init method, just like we did for the score and elapsed time.

```
05-HUD/step04/SpaceRun/RCWHUDNode.m
// ...
SKNode *powerupGroup = [SKNode node];
powerupGroup.name = @"powerupGroup";

SKLabelNode *powerupTitle = [SKLabelNode labelNodeWithFontNamed:@"AvenirNext-Bold"];
powerupTitle.fontSize = 14;
powerupTitle.fontColor = [SKColor redColor];
powerupTitle.verticalAlignmentMode = SKLabelVerticalAlignmentModeBottom;
```

```
powerupTitle.text = @"Power-up!";
powerupTitle.position = CGPointMake(0, 4);
[powerupGroup addChild:powerupTitle];

SKLabelNode *powerupValue = [SKLabelNode labelNodeWithFontNamed:@"AvenirNext-Bold"];
powerupValue.fontSize = 20;
powerupValue.fontColor = [SKColor redColor];
powerupValue.verticalAlignmentMode = SKLabelVerticalAlignmentModeTop;
powerupValue.name = @"powerupValue";
powerupValue.text = @"0s left";
powerupValue.position = CGPointMake(0, -4);
[powerupGroup addChild:powerupValue];

[self addChild:powerupGroup];

// ...
```

We build the powerupGroup node, name it so we can find it later, and add the powerupTitle and powerupValue label nodes with similar settings as we used for the other labels. Note that we're not setting the horizontal alignment at all. We're relying on the default centered horizontal alignment, which will anchor these labels properly since we're displaying this powerupGroup node in the middle of the HUD.

But we don't want this group to display when the game begins. We need to hide it until it is ready, so right after the code we typed in a moment ago, we'll set the alpha to zero.

05-HUD/step04/SpaceRun/RCWHUDNode.m
```
[self addChild:powerupGroup];
```

➤ ```
powerupGroup.alpha = 0;
```

The powerupGroup node is ready to use, but it still needs to be laid out within the RCWHUDNode's coordinate space like we did for the score and the elapsed time. Let's add these calculations in the -layoutForScene method.

**05-HUD/step04/SpaceRun/RCWHUDNode.m**
```
- (void)layoutForScene
{
    NSAssert(self.scene, @"Cannot be called unless added to a scene");
    CGSize sceneSize = self.scene.size;
    CGSize groupSize = CGSizeZero;

    SKNode *scoreGroup = [self childNodeWithName:@"scoreGroup"];
    groupSize = [scoreGroup calculateAccumulatedFrame].size;
    scoreGroup.position = CGPointMake(0 - sceneSize.width/2 + 20,
                                      sceneSize.height/2 - groupSize.height);
```
```

```
➤    SKNode *powerupGroup = [self childNodeWithName:@"powerupGroup"];
➤    groupSize = [powerupGroup calculateAccumulatedFrame].size;
➤    powerupGroup.position = CGPointMake(0,
➤                                        sceneSize.height/2 - groupSize.height);

     SKNode *elapsedGroup = [self childNodeWithName:@"elapsedGroup"];
     groupSize = [elapsedGroup calculateAccumulatedFrame].size;
     elapsedGroup.position = CGPointMake(sceneSize.width/2 - 20,
                                        sceneSize.height/2 - groupSize.height);
}
```

Just like with the scoreGroup and the elapsedGroup, we look up the powerupGroup node that contains the labels and set the position, taking the scene size into account. In this case we're setting the x-coordinate to zero, which is dead center of the node, and the y-coordinate to the top of the scene minus the calculated height of the group node.

With the power-up labels positioned and ready, we can fetch them at the start of the -showPowerupTimer: method.

05-HUD/step04/SpaceRun/RCWHUDNode.m
```
- (void)showPowerupTimer:(NSTimeInterval)time
{
    SKNode *powerupGroup = [self childNodeWithName:@"powerupGroup"];
    SKLabelNode *powerupValue =
        (SKLabelNode *)[powerupGroup childNodeWithName:@"powerupValue"];

    [powerupGroup removeActionForKey:@"showPowerupTimer"];

    // ...
}
```

We look up the powerupGroup node by its name and then find the powerupValue label by its name as a child of the powerupGroup. We could have used the child/grandchild lookup syntax with the RCWHUDNode's -childNodeWithName: method, but this works just as well, and we need both of the nodes anyway because we are updating the value label and running all the actions on the group node.

We're removing any existing action with the key named showPowerupTimer because we want to restart the timer if we're calling this method as a result of the player nabbing another power-up. Remember back in *Implementing Weapon Power-Ups with Actions*, on page 32, where we did the same thing? We're going to run the whole power-up countdown action with this key so we can restart it on the fly.

Let's continue by building the actions that form the countdown sequence.

05-HUD/step04/SpaceRun/RCWHUDNode.m
```
// ...

NSTimeInterval start = [NSDate timeIntervalSinceReferenceDate];

__weak RCWHUDNode *weakSelf = self;
SKAction *block = [SKAction runBlock:^{
    NSTimeInterval elapsed = [NSDate timeIntervalSinceReferenceDate] - start;
    NSTimeInterval left = time - elapsed;
    if (left < 0) {
        left = 0;
    }
    powerupValue.text = [NSString stringWithFormat:@"%@s left",
                            [weakSelf.timeFormatter stringFromNumber:@(left)]];
}];
SKAction *blockPause = [SKAction waitForDuration:0.05];
SKAction *countdownSequence = [SKAction sequence:@[block, blockPause]];
SKAction *countdown = [SKAction repeatActionForever:countdownSequence];

// ...
```

This countdown action repeats a sequence that runs the block of code every 0.05 seconds to update the text in the powerupValue label. We're reusing the self.timeFormatter property that we created for displaying the elapsed game time, which is why we need to use the weakSelf variable to ensure that the block does not retain self, which would lead to a retain cycle. Refer back to *Generating a Parallax Field of Stars*, on page 37, for more details about why this is necessary.

Now we can finish the -showPowerupTimer: method with the actions to fade in, fade out, and stop.

05-HUD/step04/SpaceRun/RCWHUDNode.m
```
// ...

SKAction *fadeIn = [SKAction fadeAlphaTo:1 duration:0.1];

SKAction *wait = [SKAction waitForDuration:time];
SKAction *fadeOut = [SKAction fadeAlphaTo:0 duration:1];
SKAction *stopAction = [SKAction runBlock:^{
    [powerupGroup removeActionForKey:@"showPowerupTimer"];
}];

SKAction *visuals = [SKAction sequence:@[fadeIn, wait, fadeOut, stopAction]];

[powerupGroup runAction:[SKAction group:@[countdown, visuals]]
            withKey:@"showPowerupTimer"];
```

Here we are building the visual actions. First we cause the whole powerupGroup to appear by fading in the alpha to one. Then we wait for the duration of time passed in as a method parameter. After that delay, we fade out the alpha to zero, and an action with an Objective-C block stops the entire collection of actions by calling -removeActionForKey:.

The final action run on powerupGroup is a combination of the countdown and visual actions performed in parallel. By running this action with the key showPowerupTimer, we are able to remove the action when it's done or when we need to restart the clock.

Phew! That's a lot of code. But it's nothing we haven't seen before. In the end, we're able to show the power-up countdown timer with a single method call. We can call it over and over again to restart the clock, and everything cleans up after itself when finished.

As one last piece of visual flourish, let's make the title of the power-up countdown pulse in size. Back in the -initWithSize: method, after we create the powerupGroup node and add it to the scene, we'll run this sequence of actions to make the title pulse:

`05-HUD/step04/SpaceRun/RCWHUDNode.m`
```
// ...

SKAction *scaleUp = [SKAction scaleTo:1.3 duration:0.3];
SKAction *scaleDown = [SKAction scaleTo:1 duration:0.3];

SKAction *pulse = [SKAction sequence:@[scaleUp, scaleDown]];
SKAction *pulseForever = [SKAction repeatActionForever:pulse];

[powerupTitle runAction:pulseForever];
```

We create a repeating sequence of actions that scales the node up and down by 30 percent forever. Notice that we're running this on the title itself and not the group, like we did with the actions created in the -showPowerupTimer: method. And we're never stopping it. Once we run this action on the title when the HUD is initialized, it will keep going until the node no longer exists in a scene.

We have one special scenario to consider, though. If the player collects a power-up and then immediately collides with an obstacle, the game will end, but the power-up timer will continue to show on the screen until the time is up. So in the -endGame method of the RCWHUDNode, we should remove this countdown action and fade out the timer to get rid of it.

05-HUD/step04/SpaceRun/RCWHUDNode.m

```
- (void)endGame
{
    [self removeActionForKey:@"elapsedGameTimer"];

    SKNode *powerupGroup = [self childNodeWithName:@"powerupGroup"];
    [powerupGroup removeActionForKey:@"showPowerupTimer"];

    SKAction *fadeOut = [SKAction fadeAlphaTo:0 duration:0.3];
    [powerupGroup runAction:fadeOut];
}
```

We create a fade-out action that transitions the alpha of the powerupGroup to zero over 0.3 seconds. If the node is already invisible when this is called, then nothing happens. But if the game ends shortly after the ship acquired a power-up, the message will fade away. The player won't be fooled into thinking that something is going to happen when the countdown timer is up.

All the details for animating the display are right here, and we merely have to call this method when the user collects a power-up in the RCWMyScene collision detection.

05-HUD/step04/SpaceRun/RCWMyScene.m

```
if ([ship intersectsNode:powerup]) {
    RCWHUDNode *hud = (RCWHUDNode *)[self childNodeWithName:@"hud"];
    [hud showPowerupTimer:5];
    // ...
```

We find the RCWHUDNode by name as a child of the scene, call the -showPowerup-Timer: with the duration to count down, and that's it! This fades in the display, counts down, fades out, and cleans itself up. All the work is nicely tucked away inside this special node subclass.

Next we're going to record the player's high score for posterity!

Showing the High Score

We're finished building the heads-up display, but because this is all part of showing the score to the player, we need a quick and simple high-score system. Nothing fancy, just enough to display the highest score on the main menu screen so the player can brag.

We could keep track of high scores in many ways. We could place them in a plist file in the game's documents directory or keep track of them entirely within Apple's Game Center service. To keep things simple, we'll use NSUserDefaults, where an iOS application can store preferences or configurations that should be backed up and restored along with the app.

Because the RCWHUDNode is the sole authority about the player's score, let's update the -endGame method in our RCWMyScene.m file to ask it for the score and store the value into a standard NSUserDefaults object.

05-HUD/step05/SpaceRun/RCWMyScene.m

```
- (void)endGame
{
    self.tapGesture = [[UITapGestureRecognizer alloc]
                        initWithTarget:self action:@selector(tapped)];
    [self.view addGestureRecognizer:self.tapGesture];

    RCWGameOverNode *node = [RCWGameOverNode node];
    node.position = CGPointMake(self.size.width / 2, self.size.height / 2);
    [self addChild:node];

    RCWHUDNode *hud = (RCWHUDNode *)[self childNodeWithName:@"hud"];
    [hud endGame];

➤   NSUserDefaults *defaults = [NSUserDefaults standardUserDefaults];
➤   NSNumber *highScore = [defaults valueForKey:@"highScore"];
➤   if (highScore.integerValue < hud.score) {
➤       [defaults setValue:@(hud.score) forKey:@"highScore"];
➤   }
}
```

The +standardUserDefaults class method on the NSUserDefaults returns the single instance that contains configuration data available to the game. We access it just like a dictionary, storing and retrieving values with keys. Here we're retrieving any existing high score, and if the current score in the RCWHUDNode at the end of the game is greater than the existing score, we set the new score value for the key highScore.

To show this to the player, we need to tweak the RCWMenuViewController so we have a label we can change to display the score.

05-HUD/step05/SpaceRun/RCWMenuViewController.m

```
@interface RCWMenuViewController ()
@property (nonatomic, strong) IBOutlet UISegmentedControl *difficultyChooser;
@property (nonatomic, strong) SKView *demoView;
➤ @property (nonatomic, strong) IBOutlet UILabel *highScoreLabel;
@end
```

Declaring this property as an IBOutlet makes it available in the storyboard. If you're familiar with Storyboards, wire it up to this outlet. If you'd like to use the storyboard that came with the book's sample code, grab the Main.storyboard file from the 05-HUD/step05/SpaceRun directory and replace the file in your project. For more info about Storyboards, refer back to *Customizing the Storyboard*, on page 54.

All that's left is to update the label every time the view controller is about to display by adding this method to RCWMenuViewController.m:

05-HUD/step05/SpaceRun/RCWMenuViewController.m
```
- (void)viewWillAppear:(BOOL)animated
{
    [super viewWillAppear:animated];

    NSNumberFormatter *scoreFormatter = [[NSNumberFormatter alloc] init];
    scoreFormatter.numberStyle = NSNumberFormatterDecimalStyle;

    NSUserDefaults *defaults = [NSUserDefaults standardUserDefaults];
    [defaults registerDefaults:@{@"highScore": @0}];
    NSNumber *score = [defaults valueForKey:@"highScore"];
    NSString *scoreText = [NSString stringWithFormat:@"High Score: %@",
                          [scoreFormatter stringFromNumber:score]];

    self.highScoreLabel.text = scoreText;
}
```

As a view controller subclass, the -viewWillAppear: method will be invoked just before the menu shows up on the screen, both at game launch and after the game ends. We use an NSNumberFormatter to display the score with proper formatting rules, like we did in the RCWHUDNode object, and build a string for the high-score message to set on the text property of the label.

That's it! The player's scores now live on indefinitely—well, at least on his or her iPhone.

Displaying scores is just one of many uses for heads-up displays in games. We are also displaying the elapsed time within the game and the countdown until the end of a weapon power-up. Heads-up displays could be used to display health meters or distances to destinations—anything that helps players understand their progress and reach their goals. Our game is pretty simple, like the arcade games of old.

We used forethought and math to get the nodes laid out correctly within the scene. By thinking through how you organize your node graph, you can group nodes together and lay them out relative to each other, and then lay those groups out relative to each other all the way up to the scene. Break each layout task into smaller parts, and you'll be doing awesome stuff in no time.

Our work with *Space Run* is finished. We've built a fun little game over the course of these chapters. We'll now move on to our next adventure—diving deep into the Sprite Kit physics engine and creating a pinball game!

Pinball Physics 101

Pinball is a classic game genre that uses gravity and ricochets to delight fans all over the world. As we paper prototyped back in *Physics Ball*, on page ix, we want to build a pinball game, and we want it to share some of the characteristics of its real-world counterpart. Simulating physics used to require the power of a computer the size of a small building. Sprite Kit's built-in physics engine brings this power to your pocket.

If you've never messed with a game physics engine before, have no fear. Sprite Kit's is quite powerful, yet simple enough for beginners to grasp. It integrates seamlessly with the scene graph. Any node can participate and respond to the physics calculations to give the illusion of weight, heft, bounciness, and more.

We're going to explore the Sprite Kit physics engine step by step. We'll start with a simple ball and a surface for it to bounce on. We'll slowly build up the capability to launch the ball from a plunger and restrict it to bounce around within curved walls. Because we want the pinball table to be taller than the screen and automatically scroll around, we'll also sneak in a trick to give the impression that there is a camera fixed on the ball. By the end, you'll have the basic vocabulary of the Sprite Kit physics engine and a worthy start to a fun pinball game.

Ready? Let's go!

Follow the Bouncing Ball

In this section, we're going to experiment to build a ball and plunger and then extract the nodes for the plunger and pinball into their own special SKNode subclasses.

Building any kind of physics game is a bit of a challenge. If you picked up this book and jumped in right here, you might want to at least skim the previous chapters to understand Sprite Kit's vocabulary first. You'll be leaning on a lot of accumulated knowledge and accumulating more as you go.

Download the source code for the book by following the instructions back in *How to Get the Most out of This Book*, on page xii. We'll be starting with the Xcode project in 06-Physics/step01. This is similar to the project you created when you followed the instructions to create a new project based on the Sprite Kit template back in *Setting Up a Sprite Kit Project*, on page 2. Except this one comes with all the graphics and sound files that we'll need for the pinball game ready to go. Here we'll focus on the physics engine, not setting up the Xcode project. Starting with the code in the 06-Physics/step01 directory will help you jump right into the fun stuff.

In the RCWMyScene.m file, you'll find that the -initWithSize: method used to construct the scene delegates to a second method to do the actual setup.

06-Physics/step01/PhysicsBall/RCWMyScene.m
```
- (id)initWithSize:(CGSize)size
{
    if (self = [super initWithSize:size]) {
        [self setUpScene];
    }
    return self;
}
```

Because there is so much setup to do for this game, it's easier to break it out into the -setUpScene method so we don't have so much indentation inside the if statement of -initWithSize:. For the remainder of this section, we'll be doing all our work in the -setUpScene method.

Creating a Physics Body for the Ball

Let's put a ball on a white screen. In the -setUpScene method, we'll set the background color and create a sprite node with the pinball.png image positioned in the center.

06-Physics/step01/PhysicsBall/RCWMyScene.m
```
- (void)setUpScene
{
    self.backgroundColor = [SKColor whiteColor];
    SKSpriteNode *ball = [SKSpriteNode spriteNodeWithImageNamed:@"pinball.png"];
    ball.position = CGPointMake(self.size.width/2, self.size.height/2);
    ball.size = CGSizeMake(20, 20);
    [self addChild:ball];
}
```

We first set the background color to [SKColor whiteColor], which will give good contrast to the fast-moving action of the ball. Then we create a sprite node with the pinball image texture and position it at the center of the scene's coordinates. Remember that, by default, a scene has the {0,0} origin in the bottom left of the device screen. For a refresher on Sprite Kit's coordinate system, refer back to Figure 8, *Comparing Sprite Kit and UIKit coordinates*, on page 16.

To engage the physics engine, we need to assign a physics body to the ball.

06-Physics/step01/PhysicsBall/RCWMyScene.m
```
- (void)setUpScene
{
    self.backgroundColor = [SKColor whiteColor];
    SKSpriteNode *ball = [SKSpriteNode spriteNodeWithImageNamed:@"pinball.png"];
    ball.position = CGPointMake(self.size.width/2, self.size.height/2);
    ball.size = CGSizeMake(20, 20);
    [self addChild:ball];

➤   ball.physicsBody = [SKPhysicsBody bodyWithCircleOfRadius:10];
}
```

The SKPhysicsBody objects define physics bodies within the physics world of the scene. Any node can participate in the physics simulation, but it *must* have a physics body assigned to it. Here we are using the +bodyWithCircleOfRadius: constructor method to create a specific physics body that is a circle with a 10-point radius centered around the ball.

This physics body happens to be the same size and shape as the texture of the sprite node. That's because we want a ball, after all, and it wouldn't make sense if the body were larger or smaller than what is visible.

But you can create bodies of any shape or size you want. If, say, you wanted a body that was a little smaller than the visible sprite texture, then it would give the appearance of overlapping other bodies. That's not what we want here for these nodes, but it's a useful technique to consider for your own ideas.

Build and run the game and watch what happens. The ball falls off the screen as if affected by gravity, similar to the figure shown here. But where did this gravity come from? Don't we have to set up a physics

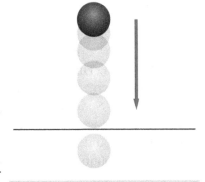

Figure 28—The ball falling off the screen

world for this to work first? That's the beauty of Sprite Kit. You have all you need to get started tinkering with the physics engine right away. Every Sprite Kit game has a physics world ready to go, yet dormant until physics bodies are assigned to nodes to start the calculations churning.

The physics world starts with a default gravity of 9.8 meters per second squared (m/s^2) in the downward direction. But we don't have to settle for that. In fact, let's change it to make the ball appear to fall slower.

06-Physics/step02/PhysicsBall/RCWMyScene.m
```
- (void)setUpScene
{
    self.backgroundColor = [SKColor whiteColor];
➤   self.physicsWorld.gravity = CGVectorMake(0, -2);
    SKSpriteNode *ball = [SKSpriteNode spriteNodeWithImageNamed:@"pinball.png"];
    ball.position = CGPointMake(self.size.width/2, self.size.height/2);
    ball.size = CGSizeMake(20, 20);
    [self addChild:ball];
    ball.physicsBody = [SKPhysicsBody bodyWithCircleOfRadius:10];
}
```

The self.physicsWorld property is always present on every SKScene object and contains an instance of SKPhysicsWorld. The gravity property on that world takes a *vector*, or a direction and magnitude, that determines the force of gravity. A CGVector is kind of like a CGPoint in that it has an x and a y component. This is saying that we want the gravity to be 2 m/s^2 in the negative, or downward, direction. Build and run the game, and you'll see the ball accelerate downward more slowly.

But we don't have to make gravity fall down. We can also make it fall diagonally up! Change the line to look like this:

```
self.physicsWorld.gravity = CGVectorMake(1, 2);
```

Now the vector says that the force of gravity should accelerate 1 m/s^2 to the right and 2 m/s^2 upward. Run the game now, and you'll see the ball "fall" up and to the right. This might seem counterintuitive at first. Shouldn't gravity always fall down? Remember, though, that games often present different points of view. *Space Run* doesn't use the physics engine and doesn't have gravity (it's in space, after all), but it uses a top-down view of the playing field. Maybe there could be a nearby planet that exerts gravity on all the nodes. Maybe gravity changes according to the tilt of the device as a game mechanic.

But this is pinball, of course. The table is supposed to be slightly slanted to allow the ball to drift toward the bottom, and you're not supposed to be able to tilt it. To establish these rules, we'll just keep the gravity fixed at 3.8 m/s^2 downward.

06-Physics/step03/PhysicsBall/RCWMyScene.m
```
self.physicsWorld.gravity = CGVectorMake(0, -3.8);
```

Why -3.8? What do meters per second squared mean in this world? Welcome to the esoteric side of physics engines. We're making this all up as we go! The physics engine tries its best to calculate how the bodies interact with each other and the world, but the result depends a lot on tinkering. All the details such as friction, mass, bounciness, and gravity come into play, and you'll find yourself tweaking values while searching for the illusion you want. When we, the authors, were experimenting with pinball physics, we came up with some reasonable numbers that made sense for the game as we saw it. (Of course, you are free to tinker away and make the pinball physics as zany as you want.)

While knowing a bit about physics in the real world would certainly be helpful, leave your PhD in physics at the door. Remember, this is an approximation for a game engine. As you'll see while we build our pinball game, we'll run into all sorts of problems that we'll have to work around and for which we'll bend the rules. Sprite Kit may bring delight to your players, but your thesis advisor might not be as impressed.

Bouncing the Ball on Another Physics Body

Let's add another body to the physics world so we can watch them interact. At the end of the -setUpScene method, we'll create a new sprite node to represent the plunger and position it below.

06-Physics/step04/PhysicsBall/RCWMyScene.m
```
- (void)setUpScene
{
    self.backgroundColor = [SKColor whiteColor];
    self.physicsWorld.gravity = CGVectorMake(0, -3.8);
    SKSpriteNode *ball = [SKSpriteNode spriteNodeWithImageNamed:@"pinball.png"];
    ball.position = CGPointMake(self.size.width/2, self.size.height/2);
    ball.size = CGSizeMake(20, 20);
    [self addChild:ball];
    ball.physicsBody = [SKPhysicsBody bodyWithCircleOfRadius:10];

➤   SKSpriteNode *plunger = [SKSpriteNode spriteNodeWithImageNamed:@"plunger.png"];
➤   plunger.position = CGPointMake(self.size.width/2, self.size.height/2 - 140);
➤   plunger.size = CGSizeMake(25, 100);
➤   [self addChild:plunger];
}
```

We're creating a sprite node with the plunger.png image texture and adding it to the scene below the ball. Run the game and watch what happens.

Figure 29—Ball falling through plunger

Whoops! The ball falls through the plunger. Remember that a node only participates in the physics simulation when it has a physics body assigned to it. Let's set that up for the plunger now.

```
06-Physics/step05/PhysicsBall/RCWMyScene.m
- (void)setUpScene
{
    self.backgroundColor = [SKColor whiteColor];

    self.physicsWorld.gravity = CGVectorMake(0, -3.8);

    SKSpriteNode *ball = [SKSpriteNode spriteNodeWithImageNamed:@"pinball.png"];
    ball.position = CGPointMake(self.size.width/2, self.size.height/2);
    ball.size = CGSizeMake(20, 20);
    [self addChild:ball];

    ball.physicsBody = [SKPhysicsBody bodyWithCircleOfRadius:10];

    SKSpriteNode *plunger = [SKSpriteNode spriteNodeWithImageNamed:@"plunger.png"];
    plunger.position = CGPointMake(self.size.width/2, self.size.height/2 - 140);
    plunger.size = CGSizeMake(25, 100);
    [self addChild:plunger];

➤   plunger.physicsBody = [SKPhysicsBody bodyWithRectangleOfSize:plunger.size];
}
```

Here we are creating a rectangular physics body of the same size as the plunger and assigning it to the plunger's physicsBody property. Rectangular bodies created in this manner are centered on the node's position. Run the game now and watch.

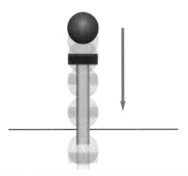

Figure 30—The plunger falls off the screen, too.

This time, *both* the plunger and the ball fall off the screen. Our plunger is now participating in the physics simulation, but it is affected by gravity, which isn't what we want. We need it to be fixed in some way. Many options exist for pinning or fixing physics body in a world, depending on the effect you're going for. For this example, let's just tell the physics body not to be affected by gravity by adding this line:

06-Physics/step06/PhysicsBall/RCWMyScene.m
```
plunger.physicsBody = [SKPhysicsBody bodyWithRectangleOfSize:plunger.size];
plunger.physicsBody.affectedByGravity = NO;
```

Now when you run the game, you'll see the plunger start out stationary, but then the ball will fall and push it off the screen. It's a very strange effect and demonstrates how odd and unnatural physics engines are. We have two bodies, both with density and heft, but only one of them is affected by gravity and has weight.

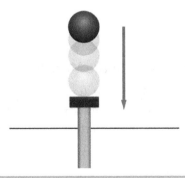

Figure 31—The ball pushes the plunger off the screen.

This isn't what we want. We need the plunger to be completely immovable by the ball. We can do that by telling Sprite Kit that this is not a *dynamic body*. We'll replace the line where we set the affectedByGravityProperty to instead look like this:

06-Physics/step07/PhysicsBall/RCWMyScene.m

```
plunger.physicsBody = [SKPhysicsBody bodyWithRectangleOfSize:plunger.size];
➤ plunger.physicsBody.dynamic = NO;
```

This tells the physics engine that the plunger's physics body should participate in the physics world as something that other bodies can bump into, but it should not be moved. It acts like a permanent fixture, screwed into the tabletop, and only participates as a place for other bodies to bounce off of. Now when you run the game, you'll see the ball fall and bounce on the top of the plunger node.

Debugging Physics Bodies

Debugging physics bodies can take some trial and error. You have to see the interaction to know whether you got it wrong. Thankfully, Sprite Kit offers some extra visual debugging aides. You can tell the SKView to highlight all the physics bodies on the screen by setting a special property in the -viewDidLoad method of the RCWViewController.m file.

```
SKView * skView = (SKView *)self.view;
skView.showsFPS = YES;
skView.showsNodeCount = YES;
➤ skView.showsPhysics = YES;
```

This serves the same purpose as the node count and frame per section display, which we first saw back in *What Just Happened?*, on page 4. By setting the showsPhysics property to YES, you'll see bounding boxes and circles drawn around all the bodies on the screen.

Adjusting Body Properties for Some More Bounce

Physics bodies according to Sprite Kit have many properties you can tweak to get the illusion you want. Let's try making the ball bounce higher, as if its core is made out of rubber. We can do that by changing the *restitution* of the ball's physics body.

06-Physics/step08/PhysicsBall/RCWMyScene.m

```
ball.physicsBody = [SKPhysicsBody bodyWithCircleOfRadius:10];
➤ ball.physicsBody.restitution = 0.9;
```

Restitution is a fancy way of saying how much force should be given or restored to the body when it collides with something else. Think of it like a percentage of the original force. Here we are saying that 90 percent of the force of collision should be the rebounding force. When you run the game, you'll see the ball bounce much, much higher—roughly 90 percent as high as it started. If you set the restitution to 1.0, then you have a *perfectly elastic collision*, as the physicists say, and the ball will bounce just as high as where you dropped it.

Of course, you don't have to restrict yourself to just numbers less than or equal to 1.0. Try changing the restitution to 1.5 and see what happens. The ball will bounce higher and higher with each collision. Eventually, the ball will bounce off the screen and take quite a while to come down for the next bounce. We've just invented Flubber![1]

It may seem odd that we'd want to *increase* energy of a body with a collision, but that's a useful mechanic in pinball. Bumpers and targets are supposed to shove the ball when hit. Old-school pinball tables use levers or springs to make that happen, but here we can achieve the illusion by increasing the restitution of a physics body. We'll make use of this later in Chapter 7, *More Physics: Paddles and Collisions*, on page 127.

Using Node Subclasses to Separate Responsibility

Before we move on to play more with the physics engine, let's take a quick moment to clean up after ourselves. Yes, we could build up the nodes and physics bodies for the rest of the game right inside the scene-implementation code, like we did for most of *Space Run*. But as the game gets more complicated, it will be harder to follow and difficult to change.

Instead, we want to break out all the components of this game into separate SKNode subclasses, each built with its own knowledge and responsibilities. They will be like black boxes that expose methods in their header files so we know how to make them talk to each other. Let's practice that now with subclasses for our ball and plunger.

Create a file named RCWPinballNode.h with these contents:

```
06-Physics/step09/PhysicsBall/RCWPinballNode.h
#import <SpriteKit/SpriteKit.h>

@interface RCWPinballNode : SKSpriteNode
+ (instancetype)ball;
@end
```

---

1.   http://en.wikipedia.org/wiki/The_Absent-Minded_Professor#Plot

Our ball node won't be doing very much during the course of the game. The main reason we want a separate subclass is so that we can isolate all the physics set up in one place. We're exposing a class method, +ball, to construct a ready-made ball node for us. Now let's build the implementation in RCWPinballNode.m.

06-Physics/step09/PhysicsBall/RCWPinballNode.m

```
#import "RCWPinballNode.h"

@implementation RCWPinballNode

+ (instancetype)ball
{
    CGFloat sideSize = 20;
    RCWPinballNode *node = [self spriteNodeWithImageNamed:@"pinball.png"];

    node.size = CGSizeMake(sideSize, sideSize);

    node.physicsBody = [SKPhysicsBody bodyWithCircleOfRadius:sideSize/2];
    node.physicsBody.restitution = 0.2;

    return node;
}

@end
```

Just as Apple exposes convenience class methods to construct nodes quickly, like the +spriteNodeWithImageNamed: method, we are writing the +ball method to build the ball with all the parameters set for us. We are setting the restitution property to a low number to decrease the bouncing. We want the ball to come to rest quickly to give the illusion that it is made out of solid metal.

In the same way, let's build the interface to a plunger node. We'll create a new file named RCWPlungerNode.h with these contents:

06-Physics/step09/PhysicsBall/RCWPlungerNode.h

```
#import <SpriteKit/SpriteKit.h>

@interface RCWPlungerNode : SKNode
@property (nonatomic) CGSize size;
+ (instancetype)plunger;
@end
```

Just like the +ball convenience constructor method on the RCWPinballNode class, we have a +plunger convenience constructor for this class. But we are also adding a special size property and making this a subclass of SKNode and not like SKSpriteNode before. To see why, create a new file named RCWPlungerNode.m with the implementation:

06-Physics/step09/PhysicsBall/RCWPlungerNode.m
```objc
#import "RCWPlungerNode.h"

@implementation RCWPlungerNode

+ (instancetype)plunger
{
    RCWPlungerNode *plunger = [self node];
    plunger.size = CGSizeMake(20, 100);

    SKSpriteNode *stick = [SKSpriteNode spriteNodeWithImageNamed:@"plunger.png"];
    stick.name = @"stick";
    stick.size = plunger.size;
    stick.position = CGPointMake(0, 0);

    stick.physicsBody = [SKPhysicsBody bodyWithRectangleOfSize:plunger.size];
    stick.physicsBody.dynamic = NO;
    stick.physicsBody.restitution = 0;

    [plunger addChild:stick];

    return plunger;
}

@end
```

The plunger node is a container node with an inner sprite node representing the stick that will be moved. And notice that we're giving the inner stick node the physics body and not the actual RCWPlungerNode itself. It won't make sense yet, but breaking things out this way helps us make this node act like a simple control that players can manipulate with their thumb. The RCWPlungerNode is a black box that promises to display a plunger. We'll add methods for grabbing and releasing the plunger when the time comes. All that responsibility will be here.

Notice that we're setting the restitution of the plunger stick's physics body to zero. When two bodies collide, the physics world takes both bodies' restitution values into account to determine the rebounding force. In this game, we want to make sure that the plunger does not affect the ball at all.

To use these in the scene, we need to add imports for the header files in the top of RCWMyScene.m.

06-Physics/step09/PhysicsBall/RCWMyScene.m
```objc
#import "RCWMyScene.h"
➤ #import "RCWPinballNode.h"
➤ #import "RCWPlungerNode.h"
```

And then we'll rewrite the -setUpScene method.

06-Physics/step09/PhysicsBall/RCWMyScene.m
```objc
- (void)setUpScene
{
    self.backgroundColor = [SKColor whiteColor];

    self.physicsWorld.gravity = CGVectorMake(0, -3.8);

    RCWPinballNode *ball = [RCWPinballNode ball];
    ball.name = @"ball";
    ball.position = CGPointMake(self.size.width/2, self.size.height/2);
    [self addChild:ball];

    RCWPlungerNode *plunger = [RCWPlungerNode plunger];
    plunger.name = @"plunger";
    plunger.position = CGPointMake(self.size.width/2, self.size.height/2 - 140);
    [self addChild:plunger];
}
```

Much cleaner! If you ran the game now, it would behave exactly as before, with the ball dropping to rest on the top of the plunger. This is a much better separation of responsibilities within the scene graph. The RCWMyScene object is responsible for instantiating and positioning the ball and plunger, but those respective nodes are responsible for setting up their own physics bodies.

Now you see how building a physics game is like playing with clay. We're experimenting one step at a time to achieve the kind of effect we want. You'll find yourself going back over the physics bodies properties, tweaking the numbers to see how things work in your own games. While the authors of this book have worked out some useful numbers for this pinball game ahead of time, tinkering in this way is how you do it.

Next, let's bring the plunger to life and follow the player's thumb.

Moving the Plunger with a Touch

Now that we have two dedicated node instances—one for the ball and one for the plunger—we can start imagining how we want to control them with the player's finger. We'll use the same kind of mechanism we did back in *Following the Finger Around*, on page 6, for *Space Run*. We need to add a dedicated property to remember the touch object when the finger is down at the top of the RCWMyScene.m file.

06-Physics/step10/PhysicsBall/RCWMyScene.m
```objc
@interface RCWMyScene ()
@property (nonatomic, weak) UITouch *plungerTouch;
@end
```

We're declaring the property as weak because we don't want to hold a strong reference to the touch. Since the touch-management system takes care of the touch objects, it will release them when the fingers leave the screen, and by using a weak reference our property will be set to nil automatically.

Next, we'll add the -touchesBegan:withEvent: method to interpret any touches and start grabbing on to the stick of the plunger.

```
06-Physics/step10/PhysicsBall/RCWMyScene.m
- (void)touchesBegan:(NSSet *)touches withEvent:(UIEvent *)event
{
    RCWPinballNode *ball = (id)[self childNodeWithName:@"ball"];
    RCWPlungerNode *plunger = (id)[self childNodeWithName:@"plunger"];
    if (self.plungerTouch == nil && [plunger isInContactWithBall:ball]) {
        UITouch *touch = [touches anyObject];
        self.plungerTouch = touch;
        [plunger grabWithTouch:touch];
    }
}
```

First, we look up the ball and the plunger in the scene graph by the names given to them when they were created and added back in the -setUpScene method. Note that we're casting the return type of the -childNodeWithName: method to id to make it easier to assign the result to the ball and plunger variables. The -childNodeWithName: method returns an object of type SKNode *. We could've written the lines more explicitly to cast the return values like this:

```
RCWPinballNode *ball = (RCWPinballNode *)[self childNodeWithName:@"ball"];
RCWPlungerNode *plunger = (RCWPlungerNode *)[self childNodeWithName:@"plunger"];
```

But because we will be using the -childNodeWithName: method a lot while building this game, we'll use the id casting shortcut to satisfy the compiler so we don't get a warning.

Once we have the ball and plunger, we check to see whether we've already assigned a touch to the self.plungerTouch property. No need to continue if we've already grabbed the plunger's stick. We also check whether the plunger is in contact with the ball by calling the -isInContactWithBall: method on RCWPlungerNode. We'll write that method in a moment. This is an example of higher-level dialogue between objects. We want this plunger object to expose methods as questions and commands that are part of its responsibility.

Assuming both of those conditions are true, we assign a touch to the self.plungerTouch property so the scene can keep track of it. Then we tell the plunger about the touch with the -grabWithTouch: method, which we'll write shortly. Again, we are planning the methods we want to write on our nodes by thinking about how our scene needs to talk to them to accomplish the goals.

Because we're in a static language with header files, we need to declare these two new methods in the RCWPlungerNode.h file so the compiler knows what to expect. Let's do that now.

06-Physics/step10/PhysicsBall/RCWPlungerNode.h

```
#import <SpriteKit/SpriteKit.h>
#import "RCWPinballNode.h"

@interface RCWPlungerNode : SKNode
@property (nonatomic) CGSize size;
+ (instancetype)plunger;

- (BOOL)isInContactWithBall:(RCWPinballNode *)ball;
- (void)grabWithTouch:(UITouch *)touch;
@end
```

We're importing the RCWPinballNode.h header file here because we'll need access to the RCWPinballNode class in our method definitions. With these declarations in place, switch to RCWPlungerNode.m and implement the -isInContactWithBall: method.

06-Physics/step10/PhysicsBall/RCWPlungerNode.m

```
- (BOOL)isInContactWithBall:(RCWPinballNode *)ball
{
    SKNode *stick = [self childNodeWithName:@"stick"];
    NSArray *contactedBodies = stick.physicsBody.allContactedBodies;
    return [contactedBodies containsObject:ball.physicsBody];
}
```

While we could do some position and frame rectangle mathematics to check to see whether the ball and the stick intersect, instead we'll use a physics engine shortcut that foreshadows our work with collisions in Chapter 7, *More Physics: Paddles and Collisions*, on page 127. Every physics body has an array of all bodies touching it through the allContactedBodies property. We first look up the stick node inside the plunger and then call -containsObject: and pass in the ball's physics body to see whether it is present. If so, then the objects are touching, and we return YES.

With that method out of the way, we add the implementation of the -grabWith-Touch: method.

06-Physics/step10/PhysicsBall/RCWPlungerNode.m

```
- (void)grabWithTouch:(UITouch *)touch
{
    CGPoint touchPoint = [touch locationInNode:self];
    SKNode *stick = [self childNodeWithName:@"stick"];

    self.yTouchDelta = stick.position.y - touchPoint.y;
}
```

We need the touch to give us the location within this plunger node's coordinate system. That's why we passed the touch into this method, so we can call -locationInNode:. Once we have the touch point, we find the stick node and note the y distance of the stick's position from the touch location. We don't want the stick to snap to the location of the thumb on the screen. We want to let the user grab anywhere, and the plunger to follow the relative downward motion.

To keep track of this coordinate delta, we need to create the yTouchDelta property in the class extension at the top of the RCWPlungerNode.m file.

06-Physics/step10/PhysicsBall/RCWPlungerNode.m
```
@interface RCWPlungerNode ()
@property (nonatomic) CGFloat yTouchDelta;
@end
```

To recap, when the touches begin, we check first to see whether the plunger is in contact with the ball. If so, then we save one of the touches in the scene's self.plungerTouch property. We tell the plunger node that it was grabbed with that touch, and the plunger calculates and saves the relative distance of the touch from the stick's current position.

Moving the Plunger in the -didSimulatePhysics Method

We're ready to write the code to actually move the plunger with the touch. Remember back in *Following the Finger Around*, on page 6, that we did not use the -touchesMoved:withEvent: callback to track motion. Because we are saving a reference of the touch object for the life of the touch, we updated the location of the spaceship in the -update: method that Sprite Kit calls on the scene once before every frame is drawn.

We want to do the same kind of thing here, but we're not supposed to update the position of nodes with physics bodies in the -update: method. Instead, we must implement the -didSimulatePhysics method in the RCWMyScene.m file, like this:

06-Physics/step10/PhysicsBall/RCWMyScene.m
```
- (void)didSimulatePhysics
{
    if (self.plungerTouch) {
        RCWPlungerNode *plunger = (id)[self childNodeWithName:@"plunger"];
        [plunger translateToTouch:self.plungerTouch];
    }
}
```

Like the -update: method, this method is also called once per frame. The difference is that this method is called after the physics simulation completes all of its calculations for this frame. We want to alter the position of the plunger after that step; otherwise, the physics simulation might compete with any changes we make in the -update: method. Apple has excellent documentation describing all the steps that take place every frame.[2] First the -update: method is called, then actions are run, the physics engine does its thing, and then -didSimulatePhysics is called for us to do any extra special work to adjust the position and properties of physics bodies before the frame is drawn.

Here we are first checking to see whether the self.plungerTouch property is set. If so, then we look up the plunger and pass that touch into the -translateToTouch: method so the plunger knows to adjust the stick to the new thumb position. We'll declare that method in the RCWPlungerNode.h header file.

06-Physics/step10/PhysicsBall/RCWPlungerNode.h
```
@interface RCWPlungerNode : SKNode
@property (nonatomic) CGSize size;
+ (instancetype)plunger;

- (BOOL)isInContactWithBall:(RCWPinballNode *)ball;
- (void)grabWithTouch:(UITouch *)touch;
- (void)translateToTouch:(UITouch *)touch;
@end
```

And then we'll implement the method in RCWPlungerNode.m.

06-Physics/step10/PhysicsBall/RCWPlungerNode.m
```
- (void)translateToTouch:(UITouch *)touch
{
    CGPoint point = [touch locationInNode:self];
    SKNode *stick = [self childNodeWithName:@"stick"];
    CGFloat newY = point.y + self.yTouchDelta;
    CGFloat plungerHeight = self.size.height;
    CGFloat upperY = 0;
    CGFloat lowerY = upperY - plungerHeight + 30;
    if (newY > upperY) {
        newY = upperY;
    } else if (newY < lowerY) {
        newY = lowerY;
    }
    stick.position = CGPointMake(0, newY);
}
```

This computes the touch location within the RCWPlungerNode's local coordinate system and calculates the newY value to reposition the plunger's visible stick based on where the thumb is. Notice how we're adding the self.yTouchDelta to

---

2. https://developer.apple.com/library/mac/documentation/GraphicsAnimation/Conceptual/CodeExplainedAdventure/
    KeepingUptoDate/KeepingUptoDate.html

the point.y value to get newY. This is taking into account that initial distance from the thumb to the position of the stick.

We're also clamping to make sure the newY value doesn't go too far above or below. We don't want the player to be able to pull the plunger's stick up and out of its track or too far down so it vanishes. Once we've properly clamped the newY value, we assign the new position to the stick node.

To recap, we give the illusion that the player is moving the plunger by checking the touch location and moving the plunger relative to the player's thumb, but only within a certain upper and lower bound.

Letting Go and Snapping the Plunger

The plunger follows the finger, but we also want it to snap in place when the touch ends. We'll switch back to RCWMyScene.m and implement the -touchesEnded:with-Event: method.

```
06-Physics/step10/PhysicsBall/RCWMyScene.m
- (void)touchesEnded:(NSSet *)touches withEvent:(UIEvent *)event
{
    if ([touches containsObject:self.plungerTouch]) {
        RCWPlungerNode *plunger = (id)[self childNodeWithName:@"plunger"];
        [plunger letGoAndLaunchBall];
    }
}
```

Like the analogous -touchesBegan:withEvent: method, this is called on the scene by the system when touches end. We ask the touches set if it happens to contain the object in the self.plungerTouch property. If so, then we find the plunger and call the method -letGoAndLaunchBall. We'll declare that method in the RCWPlungerNode.h file.

```
06-Physics/step10/PhysicsBall/RCWPlungerNode.h
- (BOOL)isInContactWithBall:(RCWPinballNode *)ball;
- (void)grabWithTouch:(UITouch *)touch;
- (void)translateToTouch:(UITouch *)touch;
➤ - (void)letGoAndLaunchBall;
```

And then we implement that method in the RCWPlungerNode.m file.

```
06-Physics/step10/PhysicsBall/RCWPlungerNode.m
- (void)letGoAndLaunchBall
{
    SKNode *stick = [self childNodeWithName:@"stick"];
    SKAction *move = [SKAction moveToY:0 duration:0.02];
    [stick runAction:move];
}
```

We look up the stick node and run a simple action to move the stick back to where it started over the span of 0.02 seconds. It's fast enough to give the kind of snap effect we want.

Phew! That took a lot of work just to get the plunger to appear to be controlled by the thumb, but it was worth it. The plunger acts like a black box that we talk to through the public methods. It knows how to start with a touch object's location, update as the touch changes, and then return the stick when we tell it that the player let go.

It's time to give this a try. Build and run the game, grab the plunger's stick, and watch it work. You'll see the ball follow the stick! As you pull it down, the ball will fall and land on top. Lift the stick up, and the ball raises up, too. You are manipulating the physics bodies in real time, and Sprite Kit is keeping up!

However, pull down the stick and watch what happens when you let go. When the action runs to snap the plunger's stick back in place, the ball snaps off to the side and falls down the screen, pulled by gravity as shown in the following figure. You can cause the same behavior if you grab the stick, pull it down, and raise it very quickly by hand.

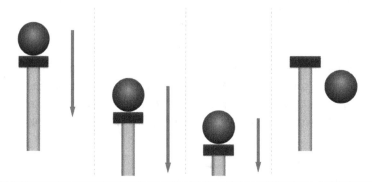

Figure 32—Moving too fast for the physics engine to keep up

What you're experiencing is one of the great frustrations of physics simulations and physics engines in general. This simulation uses discrete time steps and an ever-advancing clock to calculate where each physics body should be. Many things happen as each frame is rendered, and it is possible to confuse the physics by moving things too quickly.

When the player pulls down the plunger, the ball falls and lands on top, resting and waiting. The moment the plunger is released, the action to snap the plunger back into place kicks in and moves the plunger a large distance upward for this frame. Then the physics engine is given control and starts calculating what should happen to the physics bodies.

At this point, the physics engine sees that the plunger and the ball overlap! What is the physics engine to do? In this case the engine decides to shove the ball off to the side so that the bodies don't overlap anymore. The frame is drawn, and the next frame begins. But this time, when it is the physics engine's turn to run its calculations for the next frame, the ball is no longer on the top of the plunger. The engine then continues to plot the course of the ball as gravity takes over and it falls out of the bottom of the screen.

You'll run into this *a lot* as you experiment with physics engines. Sprite Kit is no exception. But it's not the end of the world. You can use the physics engine to your advantage! You just need to learn a bit about fixed joints to stick the ball to the top of the plunger until you let go.

Using a Fixed Joint to Stick the Ball to the Plunger

Physics bodies don't just have to drift around on their own. They can also be joined together in a variety of ways. Here, we're going to change our RCWPlungerNode so that it joins the ball to the top of the plunger when the touch begins. That joint will hold the ball in place no matter how fast the plunger moves. When the action runs to snap the plunger back in place, we will break the joint and then launch the ball by manually applying a force to it, depending on how far the player pulled down the plunger.

First, we need to change our method declarations in RCWPlungerNode.h. The plunger needs to know more details to do its new job. We have to pass it the ball and the physics world.

```
06-Physics/step11/PhysicsBall/RCWPlungerNode.h
@interface RCWPlungerNode : SKNode
@property (nonatomic) CGSize size;
+ (instancetype)plunger;

- (BOOL)isInContactWithBall:(RCWPinballNode *)ball;
➤ - (void)grabWithTouch:(UITouch *)touch
➤          holdingBall:(RCWPinballNode *)ball
➤              inWorld:(SKPhysicsWorld *)world;
- (void)translateToTouch:(UITouch *)touch;
➤ - (void)letGoAndLaunchBallInWorld:(SKPhysicsWorld *)world;
@end
```

We need the ball node and the physics world in the -grabWithTouch:holding-Ball:inWorld: method because we need to create a joint between the ball and the stick, and we need to add that joint to the physics world. We also need the physics world in the -letGoAndLaunchBallInWorld: method so we can break the joint when it's time to let go of the ball.

Let's switch to RCWPlungerNode.m and replace the old -grabWithTouch: method with the new -grabWithTouch:holdingBall:inWorld: method.

06-Physics/step11/PhysicsBall/RCWPlungerNode.m
```
- (void)grabWithTouch:(UITouch *)touch
          holdingBall:(RCWPinballNode *)ball
              inWorld:(SKPhysicsWorld *)world
{
    CGPoint touchPoint = [touch locationInNode:self];
    SKNode *stick = [self childNodeWithName:@"stick"];

    self.yTouchDelta = stick.position.y - touchPoint.y;

    CGPoint jointPoint = [self convertPoint:stick.position toNode:self.scene];

    self.jointToBall = [SKPhysicsJointFixed jointWithBodyA:stick.physicsBody
                                                     bodyB:ball.physicsBody
                                                    anchor:jointPoint];

    [world addJoint:self.jointToBall];
}
```

Where before we just set the self.yTouchDelta property, now we have to do much more. The jointPoint must be in scene coordinates, which is why we are calculating it using the -convertPoint:toNode: to take the stick's current position and return it in scene coordinates.

At the end of the method, we create an SKPhysicsJointFixed object to combine the stick.physicsBody and ball.physicsBody, anchoring them at jointPoint. We save that joint in a self.jointToBall property so we have it for later and then add that joint to the physics world with the -addJoint: method.

We don't yet have the self.jointToBall property, so we'll add it in the class extension at the top of the file.

06-Physics/step11/PhysicsBall/RCWPlungerNode.m
```
@interface RCWPlungerNode ()

@property (nonatomic) CGFloat yTouchDelta;
➤ @property (nonatomic, strong) SKPhysicsJointFixed *jointToBall;

@end
```

And now we can implement the -letGoAndLaunchBallInWorld: method to replace the old -letGoAndLaunchBall method.

06-Physics/step11/PhysicsBall/RCWPlungerNode.m

```objc
- (void)letGoAndLaunchBallInWorld:(SKPhysicsWorld *)world
{
    SKNode *stick = [self childNodeWithName:@"stick"];

    CGFloat returnY = 0;
    CGFloat distancePulled = returnY - stick.position.y;
    CGFloat forceToApply = MAX(4, distancePulled / 2);

    SKAction *move = [SKAction moveToY:returnY duration:0.02];
    SKAction *launchBall = [SKAction runBlock:^{
        [world removeJoint:self.jointToBall];
        SKPhysicsBody *ballBody = self.jointToBall.bodyB;
        [ballBody applyImpulse:CGVectorMake(0, forceToApply)];
        self.jointToBall = nil;
    }];

    SKAction *all = [SKAction sequence:@[move, launchBall]];
    [stick runAction:all];
}
```

Unlike before, where we just found the stick node and ran the action to move it in place over 0.02 seconds, we have more work to do here. We first calculate the distancePulled so we can come up with some kind of forceToApply that we will use to send the ball on its way. For this particular example, we're just using distancePulled / 2 and making sure that it is at least 4. Feel free to adjust this to taste.

Once we have the forceToApply, we build an action out of a code block that will run after the plunger stick finishes moving. This action first breaks the joint with the world's -removeJoint: method and then grabs the ball's physics body off the joint and calls -applyImpulse:, passing it a CGVector constructed with forceToApply as an upward force. Then we run this sequence of actions on the stick to move the stick back and then launch the ball.

This gives the illusion that the stick is snapping back into place and launching the ball. Because manually moving a physics body quickly can confuse the physics engine and knock the ball off, we had to improvise and bind the ball to the stick while the player's thumb is down. When the thumb lets go, we move the plunger back where it should be, break the joint, and then apply a made-up force to complete the illusion that the stick snapped into place and shoved the ball fast enough to launch it.

We still need to switch back to RCWMyScene.m and update our -touchesBegan:withEvent: and -touchesEnded:withEvent: methods to use these new method calls.

```
- (void)touchesBegan:(NSSet *)touches withEvent:(UIEvent *)event
{
    RCWPinballNode *ball = (id)[self childNodeWithName:@"ball"];
    RCWPlungerNode *plunger = (id)[self childNodeWithName:@"plunger"];

    if (self.plungerTouch == nil && [plunger isInContactWithBall:ball]) {
        UITouch *touch = [touches anyObject];
        self.plungerTouch = touch;
➤       [plunger grabWithTouch:touch holdingBall:ball inWorld:self.physicsWorld];
    }
}

- (void)touchesEnded:(NSSet *)touches withEvent:(UIEvent *)event
{
    if ([touches containsObject:self.plungerTouch]) {
        RCWPlungerNode *plunger = (id)[self childNodeWithName:@"plunger"];
➤       [plunger letGoAndLaunchBallInWorld:self.physicsWorld];
    }
}
```

And that's it. Run the game to see how it behaves. No matter how fast you move the plunger, the ball stays attached like a magnet. When you let go, the plunger launches the ball into the sky.

Pretty slick, eh? You'll be using tricks like this all the time when doing physics games. Take time to get to know how physics bodies, joints, and the world all interact together. If you run into a problem, use other rules of the physics world to help you solve it. Play along with the rules, and you won't pull your hair out in frustration.

Next, we'll build a table taller than the screen with an edge body to contain the ball and have the game automatically follow the ball like a camera moving over the table!

Building a Scrolling Table with an Edge Body

Pinball wouldn't be pinball without the familiar curved table design that guides the launched ball up and around. We want to have that same feel, so we're going to build a special kind of physics body, called an *edge body*, that will act as the walls of the table.

But more than that, we want this table to be taller than the screen and scroll to keep the ball centered. That means we need a node to contain the ball, the plunger, and all the other nodes that belong to the game. We'll reposition that special node representing the table to give the illusion of a camera following the ball.

We'll start by creating a new file named RCWTableNode.h with this class interface:

06-Physics/step12/PhysicsBall/RCWTableNode.h

```
#import <SpriteKit/SpriteKit.h>
#import "RCWPinballNode.h"

@interface RCWTableNode : SKNode
+ (instancetype)table;
- (void)followPositionOfBall:(RCWPinballNode *)ball;
@end
```

We have a convenience constructor in the +table method, just like we've done for other nodes. But we also plan to write a special method, -followPositionOfBall:, that will determine where to change the position of this table node within the scene. Again, we're building a black box with all the smarts inside—we just call methods to make it do the work.

We'll add this implementation to a new file named RCWTableNode.m to start defining our constructor.

06-Physics/step12/PhysicsBall/RCWTableNode.m

```
#import "RCWTableNode.h"

@implementation RCWTableNode

+ (instancetype)table
{
    RCWTableNode *table = [self node];

    SKShapeNode *bounds = [SKShapeNode node];
    bounds.strokeColor = [SKColor blackColor];
    [table addChild:bounds];

    // ...

    return table;
}
```

We first create an empty instance of the RCWTableNode class. Then we start setting up an SKShapeNode to use as the boundaries of the table. Shape nodes will render whatever path you give them. Here we want to use a shape node as the visual boundaries with a black color.

Next, we'll build a UIBezierPath object that will give us the shape we need.

06-Physics/step12/PhysicsBall/RCWTableNode.m

```
// ...
UIBezierPath* bezierPath = [UIBezierPath bezierPath];
[bezierPath moveToPoint: CGPointMake(0.5, -10)];
```

```
[bezierPath addCurveToPoint:CGPointMake(1, 700)
            controlPoint1:CGPointMake(0.5, -10)
            controlPoint2:CGPointMake(1, 620)];
[bezierPath addCurveToPoint:CGPointMake(160.5, 880)
            controlPoint1:CGPointMake(1, 780)
            controlPoint2:CGPointMake(45.86, 880)];
[bezierPath addCurveToPoint:CGPointMake(319, 700)
            controlPoint1:CGPointMake(275.14, 880)
            controlPoint2:CGPointMake(319, 780)];
[bezierPath addCurveToPoint:CGPointMake(319.5, -10)
            controlPoint1:CGPointMake(319, 620)
            controlPoint2:CGPointMake(319.5, -10)];

bounds.path = bezierPath.CGPath;
// ...
```

Remember back in *Creating CGPathRefs with PaintCode*, on page 27, when we used PaintCode to build a UIBezierPath object for the enemy ship to follow? We're doing the same kind of thing here. This path will give us a nice boundary that is about 900 points tall and curves around at the top. If you'd like to take a look at it, the PaintCode document used to generate this is available in 06-Physics/step12/assets/edge-path.pcvd.

The lovely thing about building this path for the SKShapeNode is that we can reuse this path for the edge body.

06-Physics/step12/PhysicsBall/RCWTableNode.m
```
// ...
bounds.physicsBody = [SKPhysicsBody bodyWithEdgeChainFromPath:bezierPath.CGPath];
// ...
```

By calling +bodyWithEdgeChainFromPath:, we build an edge body that is like an open-ended wall. Edge bodies are different from other kinds of bodies in that they are *never* dynamic, or move within the simulation. You can move them around by changing their coordinates manually, of course, but they only participate in the physics simulation as an immovable object and never budge in response to something bumping into them. They can be open ended, as we are using here, and because they allow physics bodies to move around inside of them, they make great walls or uncrossable boundaries.

Before we can use the table node in the scene, we have to import the header file at the top of the RCWMyScene.m file.

06-Physics/step12/PhysicsBall/RCWMyScene.m
```
#import "RCWMyScene.h"
#import "RCWPinballNode.h"
#import "RCWPlungerNode.h"
➤ #import "RCWTableNode.h"
```

Then, we'll start rewriting the -setUpScene method.

06-Physics/step12/PhysicsBall/RCWMyScene.m

```
- (void)setUpScene
{
    self.backgroundColor = [SKColor whiteColor];
    self.physicsWorld.gravity = CGVectorMake(0, -3.8);

➤    RCWTableNode *table = [RCWTableNode table];
➤    table.name = @"table";
➤    table.position = CGPointMake(0, 0);
➤    [self addChild:table];
    // ...
```

After setting up the background color and gravity like before, we now create an instance of our RCWTableNode, name it so we can find it later, and position it at the scene's origin at {0,0}. Next we need to change how we were setting up the plunger and ball and add them to this table node instead of the scene itself.

06-Physics/step12/PhysicsBall/RCWMyScene.m

```
RCWPlungerNode *plunger = [RCWPlungerNode plunger];
plunger.name = @"plunger";
plunger.position = CGPointMake(self.size.width - plunger.size.width/2 - 4,
                                plunger.size.height / 2);
[table addChild:plunger];
RCWPinballNode *ball = [RCWPinballNode ball];
ball.name = @"ball";
ball.position = CGPointMake(plunger.position.x,
                             plunger.position.y + plunger.size.height);
[table addChild:ball];
```

Instead of calling -addChild: on the scene object, we call it on the table. Anything that needs to scroll with the table while the game plays needs to be a child of the table. While we're at it, we're also moving the position of the plunger so it is flush on the right side of the screen, where it should be, and we position the ball so it starts out right above the plunger.

If you were to run the game right now, you'd see the thin black outline drawn on both sides of the screen where the table's boundaries are, but you wouldn't be able to control the plunger. What happened? Aren't we looking up the plunger node in the touch methods?

Well, we *were* looking them up correctly. That is, before we made the plunger and ball children of the table node. To find them as *grandchildren* of the scene, we either need to find the table node and then look for them as children of that node, or use the //nodeName syntax.

06-Physics/step12/PhysicsBall/RCWMyScene.m
```
- (void)touchesBegan:(NSSet *)touches withEvent:(UIEvent *)event
{
➤    RCWPinballNode *ball = (id)[self childNodeWithName:@"//ball"];
➤    RCWPlungerNode *plunger = (id)[self childNodeWithName:@"//plunger"];
    if (self.plungerTouch == nil && [plunger isInContactWithBall:ball]) {
        UITouch *touch = [touches anyObject];
        self.plungerTouch = touch;
        [plunger grabWithTouch:touch holdingBall:ball inWorld:self.physicsWorld];
    }
}

- (void)touchesEnded:(NSSet *)touches withEvent:(UIEvent *)event
{
    if ([touches containsObject:self.plungerTouch]) {
➤        RCWPlungerNode *plunger = (id)[self childNodeWithName:@"//plunger"];
        [plunger letGoAndLaunchBallInWorld:self.physicsWorld];
    }
}
```

This means we are asking the scene, which is self in this case, to find any
descendant that has the given name. Think of it like an XPath or a CSS
selector. We're not quite done yet because we have to change the -didSimu-
latePhysics method, too.

06-Physics/step12/PhysicsBall/RCWMyScene.m
```
- (void)didSimulatePhysics
{
➤    RCWTableNode *table = (id)[self childNodeWithName:@"table"];
➤    RCWPinballNode *ball = (id)[table childNodeWithName:@"ball"];
➤    RCWPlungerNode *plunger = (id)[table childNodeWithName:@"plunger"];
    if (self.plungerTouch) {
        [plunger translateToTouch:self.plungerTouch];
    }
➤    [table followPositionOfBall:ball];
}
```

We're handling this a bit differently. This time we are looking up the table
node and then looking up the ball and plunger as direct children of the table.
Because we need to find the table node anyway to tell it the new position of
the ball, there's no need to tell the scene to use the grandchildren selection
syntax.

Next, we need switch back to RCWTableNode.m to implement the -followPositionOfBall:
method.

06-Physics/step12/PhysicsBall/RCWTableNode.m
```
- (void)followPositionOfBall:(RCWPinballNode *)ball
{
    CGRect frame = [self calculateAccumulatedFrame];
```

```
    CGFloat sceneHeight = self.scene.size.height;
    CGFloat cameraY = ball.position.y - sceneHeight/2;
    CGFloat maxY = frame.size.height - sceneHeight;
    CGFloat minY = 0;
    if (cameraY < minY) { cameraY = minY; }
    else if (cameraY > maxY) { cameraY = maxY; }
    self.position = CGPointMake(0, 0-cameraY);
}
```

Because this is called during the -didSimulatePhysics phase of rendering the frame, we know the precise position of the ball. We calculate the frame of this table node (which includes the frame of the drawn SKShapeNode we are using to represent the boundary) and calculate the cameraY value as measured from the center of the scene to the ball's current y position. We then clamp the cameraY value to make sure the camera effect doesn't scroll past the top or bottom of the table and update the position property of this RCWTableNode to simulate a camera.

That's it! When you run the game, you'll see the ball ready and waiting on the plunger. Pull it down and let it go. The ball will scream up the side of the table, the table will change position to give the illusion of a camera following the ball, and the ball will whip around the curve at the top and then plunge down the left side on its way off into the abyss. Now that's magic.

As a minor point of concern, you'll notice that the ball picks up *a lot* of spin as it skids across the edge body of the table. High angular velocity drastically affects how the body ricochets off other bodies, and it won't work well for the kind of effect we're going for in a pinball game. Our ball is made of metal, and while it will spin a bit from friction generated by the wall, we want to dampen this effect to make it act more like we want.

Back in RCWPinballNode.m, let's add these lines to configure the ball's physics body to spin less:

06-Physics/step12/PhysicsBall/RCWPinballNode.m
```
+ (instancetype)ball
{
    CGFloat sideSize = 20;
    RCWPinballNode *node = [self spriteNodeWithImageNamed:@"pinball.png"];

    node.size = CGSizeMake(sideSize, sideSize);
    node.physicsBody = [SKPhysicsBody bodyWithCircleOfRadius:sideSize/2];
    node.physicsBody.restitution = 0.2;
➤   node.physicsBody.friction = 0.01;
➤   node.physicsBody.angularDamping = 0.5;
    return node;
}
```

The friction property does what you expect: it reduces the friction of the ball itself. The angular damping property controls how fast the ball slows down over time. These two values came from experimentation as the game progressed. Feel free to adjust to taste.

Resetting the Ball

While we're developing the game, it would be helpful if the ball would return to its rightful place at the top of the plunger once it falls off the screen. That's quite easy to check for at the end of the -didSimulatePhysics method.

06-Physics/step12/PhysicsBall/RCWMyScene.m
```
if (ball.position.y < -500) {
    ball.position = CGPointMake(plunger.position.x,
                                plunger.position.y + plunger.size.height);
    ball.physicsBody.velocity = CGVectorMake(0, 0);
    ball.physicsBody.angularVelocity = 0;
}
```

We're checking to see whether the y-coordinate of the ball's position is less than -500. That gives a nice, natural delay between the ball falling off screen and this if statement returning true. After the ball falls past that point, we immediately put it back at the top of the plunger.

We also set the linear and angular velocity of the ball's physics body to zero. This is a must because even though we changed its position to be on top of the plunger, it still has the momentum it gathered as it fell off the screen. Setting these properties to zero brings this body back to the starting state, ready to begin a new turn.

Give it a run and try it out. Perfect. Now the ball spins only slightly as it skids along the edge of the table's physics body before returning to the top of the plunger. We're playing with physics now!

And that concludes our introduction to the Sprite Kit physics engine. We've covered how to assign dynamic physics bodies to nodes, adjust their properties, push them around, attach them with joints, and constrain them within edge physics bodies. This is just the beginning. Your mind is surely spinning with ideas to try yourself. Before you head off on your own, check out the next chapter to learn how to build paddles and earn points with collisions!

More Physics: Paddles and Collisions

Our pinball game is starting to take shape, but there's a lot more we need to add before it feels like the real thing. In the previous chapter, we worked out the basics of the physics world by building a ball, the player-controlled plunger, and a table edge body that the ball rolls around.

In this chapter, we're going to build paddles as complex yet self-contained nodes combining physics bodies, joints, and forces. We'll add bumpers and targets to the scene and keep score with a heads-up display. We'll cover the ins and outs of physics body collision detection to add sound effects and animations. And we'll finish with some special adjustments to the physics of the ball in real time to keep the game playable. It's a physics extravaganza!

Ready? Let's go!

Building Paddles with Bodies, Pins, and Torque

Let's face it: we can't call this a pinball game without paddles. It's the player's sole point of control in the game (after launching the ball, of course), and we want to make it feel just right. We want paddles that appear to have weight as they snap up when triggered and fall back in place when let go. Let's think through the way a paddle is designed and see what we can use from the Sprite Kit physics toolbox to implement it.

In essence, a paddle is a bar attached to an anchor, forming a pin joint that allows it to spin around, yet it's limited in range of motion. The paddle rests at a certain angle until flipped by an angular force, causing the box to swivel around the pin to its maximum angle, as shown in the following figure.

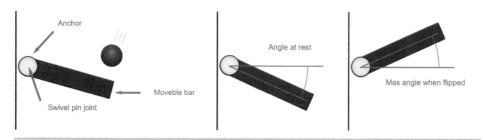

Figure 33—How paddles work

Sprite Kit includes all we need to implement this kind of mechanism using two nodes, one representing the anchor and another for the bar, and using a pin joint in the world to stick them together. We apply *torque*, or a twisting force, to the bar in an attempt to spin it. Because the bar will be pinned to the anchor node's location, the bar will appear to rotate around the anchor. We can then set properties on the pin joint to limit the range of motion. We can do this once for the left side and again for the right, and boom! We have two game paddles.

We are faced with a similar dilemma as we had back in Chapter 6, *Pinball Physics 101*, on page 99, when building the plunger. Several components will make up these paddles, but we want to hide them within a single node, exposing a clear interface for us to use from the scene. We must build a paddle node that can be reused on the left and right sides of the table, and provide a method to flip the paddles that does all the dirty work with the physics behind the scenes.

Setting Up the Paddle Node

We'll begin by creating the header file, RCWPaddleNode.h, with the following declarations:

07-MorePhysics/step01/PhysicsBall/RCWPaddleNode.h
```
#import <SpriteKit/SpriteKit.h>

typedef NS_ENUM(NSInteger, RCWPaddleSide) {
    RCWPaddleLeftSide,
    RCWPaddleRightSide
};

@interface RCWPaddleNode : SKNode
+ (instancetype)paddleForSide:(RCWPaddleSide)paddleSide;
@end
```

First, we declare an *enumerated type* to let us specify whether this paddle will be for the right side or the left side of the table. Enumerated types are how you specify a list of options for the compiler to choose from. The typedef NS_ENUM(...) statement is Apple's preferred way to do this in Objective-C. We're saying that we want a custom variable type definition, RCWPaddleSide, to be an alias of the NSInteger type, and it can be either of these two options. Because we're not explicitly initializing them, the Objective-C compiler automatically assigns 0 to the RCWPaddleLeftSide constant and 1 to RCWPaddleRightSide.

We then use that custom type in the +paddleForSide: constructor. We could have just declared the paddleSide parameter as an NSInteger and used 0 and 1 manually. But using enumerated types like this gives the compiler more hints about what we want and helps Xcode autocomplete while we type. For more information about the NS_ENUM mechanism, check out Apple's documentation.[1]

Now we'll create the implementation file, RCWPaddleNode.m, with the following contents:

07-MorePhysics/step01/PhysicsBall/RCWPaddleNode.m
```
#import "RCWPaddleNode.h"
@interface RCWPaddleNode ()
@property (nonatomic) RCWPaddleSide paddleSide;
@end

CGFloat const PaddleWidth = 120;
CGFloat const PaddleHeight = 20;

@implementation RCWPaddleNode
@end
```

We declare a private property, paddleSide, to keep track of which side this paddle was created for. We also declare a couple of CGFloat constants for the width and height of the paddle. We'll use these throughout the class definition.

Next, we'll begin writing the +paddleForSide: method to construct a new paddle.

07-MorePhysics/step01/PhysicsBall/RCWPaddleNode.m
```
+ (instancetype)paddleForSide:(RCWPaddleSide)paddleSide
{
    RCWPaddleNode *paddle = [RCWPaddleNode node];
    paddle.paddleSide = paddleSide;
    // ...

    return paddle;
}
```

---

1. https://developer.apple.com/library/ios/releasenotes/ObjectiveC/ModernizationObjC/AdoptingModernObjective-C/AdoptingModernObjective-C.html#//apple_ref/doc/uid/TP40014150-CH1-SW6

Just like we've done before in Chapter 6, *Pinball Physics 101*, on page 99, we use the standard node constructor to give us a blank instance of RCWPaddleNode that we set up and return in this constructor. Because we need to keep track of the paddle side, we assign it to the paddleSide property.

But of course, this node doesn't show anything yet. Next we add the two child sprite nodes for the bar and the anchor.

```
07-MorePhysics/step01/PhysicsBall/RCWPaddleNode.m
SKSpriteNode *bar = [SKSpriteNode spriteNodeWithImageNamed:@"paddle-box"];
bar.name = @"bar";
bar.size = CGSizeMake(PaddleWidth, PaddleHeight);
[paddle addChild:bar];

SKSpriteNode *anchor = [SKSpriteNode spriteNodeWithImageNamed:@"paddle-anchor"];
anchor.name = @"anchor";
anchor.size = CGSizeMake(PaddleHeight, PaddleHeight);
[paddle addChild:anchor];
```

We build two sprite nodes with their image textures and appropriate sizes before adding them to the paddle as child nodes. We haven't set their positions yet. That's because it depends on whether this paddle node will be used for the left or the right side.

```
07-MorePhysics/step01/PhysicsBall/RCWPaddleNode.m
if (paddle.paddleSide == RCWPaddleRightSide) {
    bar.position = CGPointMake(0-PaddleWidth/2, 0);
    anchor.position = CGPointMake(bar.position.x + bar.size.width/2, 0);
} else {
    bar.position = CGPointMake(PaddleWidth/2, 0);
    anchor.position = CGPointMake(bar.position.x - bar.size.width/2, 0);
}
```

If the paddleSide property is equal to the RCWPaddleRightSide constant, then we place the bar so it sticks out to the left with the anchor positioned over the right end of the bar. Otherwise, we do the opposite for the left paddle.

We finish the method by building the physics bodies for the box and anchor.

```
07-MorePhysics/step01/PhysicsBall/RCWPaddleNode.m
CGFloat anchorRadius = anchor.size.width/2;
anchor.physicsBody = [SKPhysicsBody bodyWithCircleOfRadius:anchorRadius];
anchor.physicsBody.dynamic = NO;

bar.physicsBody = [SKPhysicsBody bodyWithRectangleOfSize:bar.size];
bar.physicsBody.mass = 0.05;
bar.physicsBody.restitution = 0.1;
bar.physicsBody.angularDamping = 0;
bar.physicsBody.friction = 0.02;
```

We build a circular physics body for the anchor by calculating the radius based on the size, and we make sure to set the dynamic property to NO because we do *not* want this anchor to move or be moved in the scene.

The bar's physics body has a mass of 0.05 to make it light and easy to push by the player. A low restitution ensures the ball won't bounce much. Angular damping controls how much the rotation of an object slows down over time. We don't want that at all, so we're setting it to zero. And finally, we set the friction of the bar to 0.02 to make sure that flicking the ball doesn't impart too much spin. This is for the same reason we reduced the friction of the table's edge body back in *Building a Scrolling Table with an Edge Body*, on page 120.

Let's now add two paddle nodes to the scene. Switch over to the RCWMyScene.m file and import the header file at the top.

07-MorePhysics/step01/PhysicsBall/RCWMyScene.m
```
#import "RCWMyScene.h"
#import "RCWPinballNode.h"
#import "RCWPlungerNode.h"
#import "RCWTableNode.h"
➤ #import "RCWPaddleNode.h"
```

Then we'll add the paddles to the scene at the bottom of the -setUpScene method.

07-MorePhysics/step01/PhysicsBall/RCWMyScene.m
```
RCWPaddleNode *leftPaddle = [RCWPaddleNode paddleForSide:RCWPaddleLeftSide];
leftPaddle.name = @"leftPaddle";
leftPaddle.position = CGPointMake(9, 100);
[table addChild:leftPaddle];

RCWPaddleNode *rightPaddle = [RCWPaddleNode paddleForSide:RCWPaddleRightSide];
rightPaddle.name = @"rightPaddle";
rightPaddle.position = CGPointMake(plunger.position.x -
                                   plunger.size.width - 1, 100);
[table addChild:rightPaddle];
```

We create one paddle for the left and one for the right, remembering to use the proper RCWPaddleSide enumerated type constants in the constructor. We name them to find them later, position them on the left and right sides, and add them as children to the RCWTableNode.

If you build and run the game right now, you'll see the paddles start on the table in the right spot, but then the boxes fall while pulled by gravity. We need to set up the pin joint to fix the boxes at the position of the anchor nodes. We'll switch back to RCWPaddleNode.h and add a method definition we can call to make that happen.

```
07-MorePhysics/step02/PhysicsBall/RCWPaddleNode.h
@interface RCWPaddleNode : SKNode
+ (instancetype)paddleForSide:(RCWPaddleSide)paddleSide;
➤ - (void)createPinJointInWorld;
@end
```

Then we'll begin implementing the method in the RCWPaddleNode.m file.

```
07-MorePhysics/step02/PhysicsBall/RCWPaddleNode.m
- (void)createPinJointInWorld
{
    NSAssert(self.scene, @"Can only create joint when placed in scene.");

    SKNode *bar = [self childNodeWithName:@"bar"];
    SKNode *anchor = [self childNodeWithName:@"anchor"];

    // ...

}
```

The first line asserts that the scene property of this node is not nil, similar to what we did in the -layoutForScene method back in *Aligning Label Nodes Within Groups*, on page 80. This method can only do its work after the paddle has been added to the scene. This NSAssert() call is a sanity check during development. If we ever forget, then the app will crash and complain about it loudly.

Now we'll build the pin joint between the bar and anchor node physics bodies in the scene.

```
07-MorePhysics/step02/PhysicsBall/RCWPaddleNode.m
- (void)createPinJointInWorld
{
    NSAssert(self.scene, @"Can only create joint when placed in scene.");

    SKNode *bar = [self childNodeWithName:@"bar"];
    SKNode *anchor = [self childNodeWithName:@"anchor"];

➤   CGPoint positionInScene = [self convertPoint:anchor.position toNode:self.scene];
➤   SKPhysicsJointPin *pin = [SKPhysicsJointPin jointWithBodyA:bar.physicsBody
➤                                                         bodyB:anchor.physicsBody
➤                                                        anchor:positionInScene];
➤   pin.shouldEnableLimits = YES;
➤   pin.lowerAngleLimit = -0.5;
➤   pin.upperAngleLimit = 0.5;
➤
➤   [self.scene.physicsWorld addJoint:pin];
}
```

Similar to how we built the fixed joint back in *Using a Fixed Joint to Stick the Ball to the Plunger*, on page 117, we look up the anchor's position in the scene's coordinates and construct an instance of SKPhysicsJointPin, passing in the two bodies and the scene anchor point. A pin joint allows the bodies to be locked together, yet rotate around a common point. But since the anchor node has its dynamic property set to NO, only the bar will rotate. We want to limit the range of motion, so we set the shouldEnableLimits property on the pin joint to YES and then set the upper and lower angle limits in radians.

We have the joint object; now we need to add it to the world. If you remember back in *Using a Fixed Joint to Stick the Ball to the Plunger*, on page 117, we passed the physics world into the method that set up the plunger's joint. That's a perfectly valid way to do it, but we're doing it differently here. Every node has access to the scene it belongs to with the scene property. And the scene exposes the ever-present world in the physicsWorld property. Here we are reaching through the scene to the physics world and adding the joint directly.

Why would you choose to do one over the other? As with all programming, it helps to be explicit. While reaching through the scene to get access to the physics world is convenient, it can also obscure the intent. When you are trying to debug joint problems in the scene, can you glance at the method names and figure out what's happening? In the case of the plunger, passing in the physics world explicitly helps communicate that we are going to use it to add the joint. In this -createPinJointInWorld method, we named it such that anyone who sees it knows that it does something with joints in the physics world. Whichever means you choose, make sure you name your methods and parameters in a way that helps you discern what's going on as you read them. It helps keep you organized as the code grows.

We'll switch back to the RCWMyScene.m file and change where we add the paddles to the scene in the -setUpScene method to now call the -createPinJointInWorld method.

07-MorePhysics/step02/PhysicsBall/RCWMyScene.m

```
RCWPaddleNode *leftPaddle = [RCWPaddleNode paddleForSide:RCWPaddleLeftSide];
leftPaddle.name = @"leftPaddle";
leftPaddle.position = CGPointMake(9, 100);
[table addChild:leftPaddle];
```

➤ `[leftPaddle createPinJointInWorld];`

```
RCWPaddleNode *rightPaddle = [RCWPaddleNode paddleForSide:RCWPaddleRightSide];
rightPaddle.name = @"rightPaddle";
rightPaddle.position = CGPointMake(plunger.position.x -
                                   plunger.size.width - 1, 100);
[table addChild:rightPaddle];
```

➤ `[rightPaddle createPinJointInWorld];`

Build and run the application now, and you'll see the paddles properly pinned and gracefully fall to their resting angle as gravity pulls them down at the start of the game!

Flipping the Paddles with Torque

Obviously, these paddles are useless until players can control them by touch. Let's switch back to the RCWPaddleNode.h file and add a method definition in the header for a simple flip.

07-MorePhysics/step03/PhysicsBall/RCWPaddleNode.h
```
@interface RCWPaddleNode : SKNode

+ (instancetype)paddleForSide:(RCWPaddleSide)paddleSide;
- (void)createPinJointInWorld;
➤ - (void)flip;

@end
```

Then, we'll switch to RCWPaddleNode.m and add the method definition that applies torque to make the paddle spin.

07-MorePhysics/step03/PhysicsBall/RCWPaddleNode.m
```
- (void)flip
{
    SKNode *bar = [self childNodeWithName:@"bar"];
    CGFloat torque = 3;
    if (self.paddleSide == RCWPaddleRightSide) {
        torque *= -1;
    }
    [bar.physicsBody applyTorque:torque];
}
```

We fetch the bar node as a child by its name. Then we mark the amount of torque we want to apply in the torque variable. If the paddle is on the right side, then we multiply torque by −1 to make it negative, since the force would need to spin the paddle in the other direction. Then we spin the paddle box's physics body with the -applyTorque: method. Because the body is pinned, it will spin around the anchor point in the scene. Because we set the upper angle limit, it will stop at just the right spot no matter how much force we apply.

Let's switch back to the RCWMyScene.m file. We want to track whether the user is holding his finger down on the left and right sides of the screen, so we'll handle this similarly to the way we controlled the spaceship's movement back in Chapter 1, *Introduction to Sprite Kit*, on page 1. We'll add two new touch properties to the scene's class extension.

07-MorePhysics/step03/PhysicsBall/RCWMyScene.m
```
@interface RCWMyScene ()
@property (nonatomic, weak) UITouch *plungerTouch;
➤ @property (nonatomic, weak) UITouch *leftPaddleTouch;
➤ @property (nonatomic, weak) UITouch *rightPaddleTouch;
@end
```

Then we need to set these properties in the -touchesBegan:withEvent: method, but only if we're not already handling touches for the plunger.

07-MorePhysics/step03/PhysicsBall/RCWMyScene.m
```
- (void)touchesBegan:(NSSet *)touches withEvent:(UIEvent *)event
{
    RCWPinballNode *ball = (id)[self childNodeWithName:@"//ball"];
    RCWPlungerNode *plunger = (id)[self childNodeWithName:@"//plunger"];

    if (self.plungerTouch == nil && [plunger isInContactWithBall:ball]) {
        UITouch *touch = [touches anyObject];
        self.plungerTouch = touch;
        [plunger grabWithTouch:touch holdingBall:ball inWorld:self.physicsWorld];
➤   } else {
➤       for (UITouch *touch in touches) {
➤           CGPoint where = [touch locationInNode:self];
➤           if (where.x < self.size.width/2) {
➤               self.leftPaddleTouch = touch;
➤           } else {
➤               self.rightPaddleTouch = touch;
➤           }
➤       }
➤   }
}
```

We've added everything for the paddles under the else clause so that the paddles respond only if the plunger isn't active. We loop over all the touches on the screen, because we need to handle touches that count for the right and left side at the same time. For each touch we check to see whether it is on the left half of the scene or the right, and assign the touch objects to their respective properties.

We've kept track of the touches; now we have to do the work to actually flip. Because we want to apply the forces to the paddle *before* the rest of the physics engine runs its calculations for the frame, we'll add an -update: method.

07-MorePhysics/step03/PhysicsBall/RCWMyScene.m
```
- (void)update:(NSTimeInterval)currentTime
{
    if (self.leftPaddleTouch) {
        RCWPaddleNode *leftPaddle = (id)[self childNodeWithName:@"//leftPaddle"];
        [leftPaddle flip];
    }
```

```
    if (self.rightPaddleTouch) {
        RCWPaddleNode *rightPaddle = (id)[self childNodeWithName:@"//rightPaddle"];
        [rightPaddle flip];
    }
}
```

If the left or right paddle touch properties are set, we'll find that respective paddle in the scene using the //nodeName grandchild syntax and tell the paddle to flip. Boom.

Remember back in *Moving the Plunger in the -didSimulatePhysics Method*, on page 113, when we talked about the order of operations that Sprite Kit performs for every frame? The -update: method is called first; the physics engine runs calculations for the frame and then calls the -didSimulatePhysics method. Here we want the flipping force to matter in this frame's physics calculations. That's why we must do this work in the -update: method instead.

Build and run the game. Try to keep the ball up and in the air!

We built our paddles out of two nodes with physics bodies and a pin joint anchoring them. We flipped the box nodes with a torque force, which forces them to rotate around the pin joint, and we limited the range of motion with the upper and lower angle limits on the pin. We ended up with a node that we can reuse and position on both sides of the table.

Whacking the ball around in an empty space is kind of boring. Let's add targets and bumpers next!

Loading Targets and Bumpers from a Layout File

It's time to build the other elements of classic pinball games: rectangular bumpers that block and repel the ball when hit, and circular targets that also repel the ball but add points to the player's score.

Up to this point, we've been hard-coding all of our node positions. For a pinball game, you might want to have different layouts for the player to choose from —each with its own unique challenge. Let's solve that by giving the table node the power to load layouts of targets and bumpers from configuration files.

Specifically, we're going to use the *property list*, or *plist*, format which is Apple's standard storage mechanism for simple arrays and dictionaries of values. Xcode includes a nice plist editor, which will come in handy for us.

Let's start by building the bumper and target node classes. We'll create a file named RCWBumperNode.h with these contents:

07-MorePhysics/step04/PhysicsBall/RCWBumperNode.h
```
#import <SpriteKit/SpriteKit.h>

@interface RCWBumperNode : SKSpriteNode
+ (instancetype)bumperWithSize:(CGSize)size;
@end
```

Our bumper is a subclass of SKSpriteNode with a constructor method to build a bumper of arbitrary size that stretches the texture to fit. Let's create the corresponding RCWBumperNode.m file.

07-MorePhysics/step04/PhysicsBall/RCWBumperNode.m
```
#import "RCWBumperNode.h"

@implementation RCWBumperNode

+ (instancetype)bumperWithSize:(CGSize)size
{
    RCWBumperNode *bumper = [self spriteNodeWithImageNamed:@"bumper"];
    bumper.size = size;
    bumper.physicsBody = [SKPhysicsBody bodyWithRectangleOfSize:size];
    bumper.physicsBody.dynamic = NO;
    bumper.physicsBody.restitution = 2;

    return bumper;
}
@end
```

We build the node by calling the -spriteNodeWithImageNamed: method with the image texture we want and set the size to the size parameter passed into this constructor. When building the physics body, we set the dynamic property to NO to make this a static body because we don't ever want the bumper to move when hit by the ball.

We also set the restitution to 2 because we want the bumper to impart more bounce to the ball when hit. We first discussed this back in *Adjusting Body Properties for Some More Bounce*, on page 106. Any value greater than 1 gives more energy to the moving bodies after a collision. This mimics the behavior of real pinball bumpers that use levers to propel the ball when struck.

Next, we'll create the RCWTargetNode.h header file for the target nodes.

07-MorePhysics/step04/PhysicsBall/RCWTargetNode.h
```
#import <SpriteKit/SpriteKit.h>

@interface RCWTargetNode : SKSpriteNode
+ (instancetype)targetWithRadius:(CGFloat)radius;
@property (nonatomic) NSInteger pointValue;
@end
```

This is almost the same as what we did for the RCWBumperNode class, but we're creating targets with a radius to make them circular, and we are adding a pointValue property that we'll set when we load the target from the configuration file. Once we cover scoring for this game in *Responding to Collisions*, on page 148, we'll use this point value property to add to the player's score.

Now let's implement the class constructor in a new file named RCWTargetNode.m.

07-MorePhysics/step04/PhysicsBall/RCWTargetNode.m

```
#import "RCWTargetNode.h"

@implementation RCWTargetNode

+ (instancetype)targetWithRadius:(CGFloat)radius
{
    RCWTargetNode *target = [self spriteNodeWithImageNamed:@"target"];
    target.size = CGSizeMake(radius*2, radius*2);

    target.physicsBody = [SKPhysicsBody bodyWithCircleOfRadius:radius];
    target.physicsBody.dynamic = NO;
    target.physicsBody.restitution = 2;

    return target;
}

@end
```

This is similar to the bumpers. We create the node instance with an image texture, set the size based on the radius, and build a static physics body with a restitution of two so the ball bounces off with more force.

We want to add these to the table. To make it easy to load different configurations, let's start by changing the table node's interface header in RCWTableNode.h to add the method that will load a layout from a filename in the app bundle.

07-MorePhysics/step04/PhysicsBall/RCWTableNode.h

```
@interface RCWTableNode : SKNode
+ (instancetype)table;
- (void)followPositionOfBall:(RCWPinballNode *)ball;
➤ - (void)loadLayoutNamed:(NSString *)name;
@end
```

Then we'll import the target and bumper node class headers in RCWTableNode.m.

07-MorePhysics/step04/PhysicsBall/RCWTableNode.m

```
  #import "RCWTableNode.h"
➤ #import "RCWBumperNode.h"
➤ #import "RCWTargetNode.h"
```

Now let's begin to implement the -loadLayoutNamed: method in the RCWTableNode.m file.

07-MorePhysics/step04/PhysicsBall/RCWTableNode.m

```
- (void)loadLayoutNamed:(NSString *)name
{
    NSURL *layoutPath = [[NSBundle mainBundle] URLForResource:name
                                                withExtension:@"plist"];
    NSDictionary *layout = [NSDictionary dictionaryWithContentsOfURL:layoutPath];
    // ...


}
```

In similar fashion to the way we loaded particle emitter files back in *Loading Particle Emitter Files*, on page 45, we're fetching the full path to the layout file in the application bundle. Then we use the [NSDictionary dictionaryWithContentsOfURL:] method to construct a simple NSDictionary from the data in the file.

What do these files look like? They are XML files that define arrays and dictionaries of simple values such as numbers, strings, and dates. While you follow along, we are using the plist file at 07-MorePhysics/step04/PhysicsBall/layout.plist in the source code that comes with the book. The beginning of it looks like this when you view it as XML:

```
<?xml version="1.0" encoding="UTF-8"?>
<!DOCTYPE plist PUBLIC "-//Apple//DTD PLIST 1.0//EN">
<plist version="1.0">
<dict>
  <key>bumpers</key>
  <array>
    <dict>
      <key>x</key>
      <integer>90</integer>
      <key>y</key>
      <integer>780</integer>
      <key>width</key>
      <integer>70</integer>
      <key>height</key>
      <integer>10</integer>
      <key>degrees</key>
      <integer>-18</integer>
    </dict>
    <!- ... ->
```

But Xcode offers a nice editor for property list files. If you open the file in Xcode, it will look like the following figure:

Key		Type	Value
▼ Root		Dictionary	(2 items)
▼ bumpers		Array	(4 items)
▼ Item 0		Dictionary	(5 items)
x		Number	90
y		Number	780
width		Number	70
height		Number	10
degrees		Number	–18
▼ Item 1	⊕ ⊖	Dictionary	(5 items)
x		Number	230
y		Number	750
width		Number	70

Figure 34—Xcode's property list editor

This editor lets you easily tweak values. For more information about property lists and how to edit them, check out Apple's documentation.[2] Throughout the rest of this chapter, you can get access to the property list files in each step of the sample code.

Back in the -loadLayoutNamed: method in the RCWTableNode.m file, we have the layout loaded into an NSDictionary. All we have to do is access the array of bumpers, loop over them, and create the proper nodes.

07-MorePhysics/step04/PhysicsBall/RCWTableNode.m
```
for (NSDictionary *bumperConfig in layout[@"bumpers"]) {
    CGSize size = CGSizeMake([bumperConfig[@"width"] floatValue],
                             [bumperConfig[@"height"] floatValue]);
    CGPoint position = CGPointMake([bumperConfig[@"x"] floatValue],
                                   [bumperConfig[@"y"] floatValue]);
    RCWBumperNode *bumper = [RCWBumperNode bumperWithSize:size];
    bumper.position = position;
    bumper.zRotation = [bumperConfig[@"degrees"] floatValue] * M_PI / 180;
    [self addChild:bumper];
}
```

The root of the plist file defines a dictionary with the keys bumpers and targets that both contain arrays of dictionaries defining the properties we'll set on the respective nodes. For each of the bumper configuration dictionaries, we access the different values within and create the proper size, position, and rotation to set up a bumper node. The width, height, x, and y coordinates are simple floating-point values, and we use the -floatValue method on NSNumber to get the CGFloat results that CGSizeMake() and CGPointMake() require.

---

2. https://developer.apple.com/library/mac/documentation/Cocoa/Conceptual/PropertyLists/Introduction/Introduction.html#//apple_ref/doc/uid/10000048i

Note that we're taking the value in degrees and multiplying it by M_PI/180 to convert it into radians. The angle in the plist file is specified in degrees because it's easier for humans to work with, but the zRotation property requires radians.

Next, we'll add a for loop to build the RCWTargetNode objects from the layout.

07-MorePhysics/step04/PhysicsBall/RCWTableNode.m
```
for (NSDictionary *targetConfig in layout[@"targets"]) {
    CGFloat radius = [targetConfig[@"radius"] floatValue];
    CGPoint position = CGPointMake([targetConfig[@"x"] floatValue],
                                   [targetConfig[@"y"] floatValue]);
    RCWTargetNode *target = [RCWTargetNode targetWithRadius:radius];
    target.position = position;
    target.pointValue = [targetConfig[@"pointValue"] floatValue];
    [self addChild:target];
}
```

This is the same process we went through for the bumpers, except that instead of assigning an angle of rotation, we retrieve the point value from the dictionary and assign it to the target's pointValue property.

The scene object needs to call this method, so let's switch back to RCWMyScene.m and add this line after adding the table.

07-MorePhysics/step04/PhysicsBall/RCWMyScene.m
```
RCWTableNode *table = [RCWTableNode table];
table.name = @"table";
table.position = CGPointMake(0, 0);
[self addChild:table];
```

➤ `[table loadLayoutNamed:@"layout"];`

Build the game and run it to see how it works. We have a fully populated level with targets and bumpers!

Property list files are a very simple way to store configuration information for all sorts of parts in your games. You could include many different level layouts and even build more kinds of nodes that the ball can bump into. Your imagination is the only limit.

Showing the Score in a Heads-Up Display

The targets are on the table, but we're not tracking or displaying the score anywhere. Let's add a simple heads-up display, similar to what we did for the *Space Run* game back in Chapter 5, *Keeping Score with a Heads-Up Display*, on page 77. We don't need nearly as much complexity as we did then. There's no timer. We just need to show and increase the score.

Let's create a file named RCWHUDNode.h with the following header:

07-MorePhysics/step04/PhysicsBall/RCWHUDNode.h

```
#import <SpriteKit/SpriteKit.h>
@interface RCWHUDNode : SKNode
@property (nonatomic) NSInteger score;
+ (instancetype)hud;
- (void)layoutForScene;
- (void)addPoints:(NSInteger)points;
@end
```

We're declaring a property to keep track of the score, a constructor method, a method to lay out the internal label nodes once in the scene, and a method to add points to the score. Now we'll create a file named RCWHUDNode.m with the class implementation and constructor.

07-MorePhysics/step04/PhysicsBall/RCWHUDNode.m

```
#import "RCWHUDNode.h"
@interface RCWHUDNode ()
@property (nonatomic, strong) NSNumberFormatter *scoreFormatter;
@end
@implementation RCWHUDNode
+ (instancetype)hud
{
    RCWHUDNode *hud = [self node];
    SKNode *scoreGroup = [SKNode node];
    scoreGroup.name = @"scoreGroup";
    SKLabelNode *scoreTitle =
        [SKLabelNode labelNodeWithFontNamed:@"AvenirNext-Medium"];
    scoreTitle.fontSize = 12;
    scoreTitle.fontColor = [SKColor blackColor];
    scoreTitle.verticalAlignmentMode = SKLabelVerticalAlignmentModeBottom;
    scoreTitle.text = @"SCORE";
    scoreTitle.position = CGPointMake(0, 4);
    [scoreGroup addChild:scoreTitle];

    SKLabelNode *scoreValue =
        [SKLabelNode labelNodeWithFontNamed:@"AvenirNext-Bold"];
    scoreValue.fontSize = 20;
    scoreValue.fontColor = [SKColor blackColor];
    scoreValue.verticalAlignmentMode = SKLabelVerticalAlignmentModeTop;
    scoreValue.name = @"scoreValue";
    scoreValue.text = @"0";
    scoreValue.position = CGPointMake(0, -4);

    [scoreGroup addChild:scoreValue];
    [hud addChild:scoreGroup];
    hud.scoreFormatter = [[NSNumberFormatter alloc] init];
    hud.scoreFormatter.numberStyle = NSNumberFormatterDecimalStyle;
    return hud;
}
@end
```

Again, it's very similar to the process we went through to create the *Space Run* game heads-up display. We have a node acting as a group for the score title and score value, and we're using a number formatter for all the thousands separator goodies.

These nodes need to be positioned once the HUD is added to the scene, so let's build the -layoutForScene method next.

07-MorePhysics/step04/PhysicsBall/RCWHUDNode.m
```
- (void)layoutForScene
{
    NSAssert(self.scene, @"Cannot be called unless added to a scene");
    CGSize sceneSize = self.scene.size;
    SKNode *scoreGroup = [self childNodeWithName:@"scoreGroup"];
    CGSize groupSize = [scoreGroup calculateAccumulatedFrame].size;
    scoreGroup.position = CGPointMake(0, sceneSize.height/2 - groupSize.height);
}
```

We assert that the scene property is set because this method is useless otherwise. Then we find the score group and position it in the middle of the scene.

Next, let's write the method to add points to the score.

07-MorePhysics/step04/PhysicsBall/RCWHUDNode.m
```
- (void)addPoints:(NSInteger)points
{
    self.score += points;
    SKLabelNode *scoreValue = (id)[self childNodeWithName:@"scoreGroup/scoreValue"];
    scoreValue.text = [self.scoreFormatter stringFromNumber:@(self.score)];
    SKAction *scale = [SKAction scaleTo:1.5 duration:0.02];
    SKAction *shrink = [SKAction scaleTo:1 duration:0.07];
    SKAction *all = [SKAction sequence:@[scale, shrink]];
    [scoreValue runAction:all];
}
```

We first add the points to the score property, then we find the scoreValue label node using the "scoreGroup/scoreValue" grandchild search syntax. We update the text of the label with the new score and then run a quick scaling action for some visual flourish.

We're ready to add and use the HUD, so let's switch back over the RCWMyScene.m file and import the RCWHUDNode.h header at the top.

07-MorePhysics/step04/PhysicsBall/RCWMyScene.m
```
  #import "RCWMyScene.h"
  #import "RCWPinballNode.h"
  #import "RCWPlungerNode.h"
  #import "RCWTableNode.h"
  #import "RCWPaddleNode.h"
➤ #import "RCWHUDNode.h"
```

Then, at the bottom of the -setUpScene method, we'll add the code to create and position the HUD.

07-MorePhysics/step04/PhysicsBall/RCWMyScene.m
```
RCWHUDNode *hud = [RCWHUDNode hud];
hud.name = @"hud";
hud.position = CGPointMake(self.size.width/2, self.size.height/2);
[self addChild:hud];
[hud layoutForScene];
```

We build the HUD node, name it so we can find it later, position it in the center, and add it to the scene. Note that we're adding it to the scene and *not to the table node*, like the rest of the elements of the game. Remember that the table node pans around like a camera following the ball. We don't want that to happen with the HUD. We want it fixed at the top.

We have the HUD node in the top of the scene, ready to display the points. But we have a problem: how do we know if the ball hit a target? We must turn our attention to the power of Sprite Kit's collision detection!

Detecting Collisions Between Bodies

Up to this point, the physics engine has been handling collisions and contact between the bodies for us on its own. We haven't needed to intervene in any way. But now we have to. We want to be notified when the ball hits a target so we can increase the score. We also want to know when the ball hits either a target or a bumper so we can display some special effects and play sounds.

That's where the category bitmasks and the contact delegate comes in. By the end of this section, you'll know how to tell Sprite Kit which collisions you care about.

First, let's register our scene object as the contact delegate to get told when physics bodies collide with each other. In the RCWMyScene.m file, change the class extension to declare that this class implements the SKPhysicsContactDelegate protocol.

07-MorePhysics/step05/PhysicsBall/RCWMyScene.m
```
@interface RCWMyScene ()
➤ <SKPhysicsContactDelegate>
@property (nonatomic, weak) UITouch *plungerTouch;
@property (nonatomic, weak) UITouch *leftPaddleTouch;
@property (nonatomic, weak) UITouch *rightPaddleTouch;
@end
```

The *delegate pattern* is used all over Apple's frameworks. Delegates let you extend a class's normal behavior. In this case, the physics world handles contacts between physics bodies for us, but we want to extend that behavior and do extra things. For our scene to play that role, it must declare to the compiler that it implements the SKPhysicsContactDelegate protocol.

Now let's change the -setUpScene method to assign the scene as the contact delegate of the physics world.

07-MorePhysics/step05/PhysicsBall/RCWMyScene.m

```
- (void)setUpScene
{
    self.backgroundColor = [SKColor whiteColor];
    self.physicsWorld.gravity = CGVectorMake(0, -3.8);
➤    self.physicsWorld.contactDelegate = self;
    // ...
```

Our scene is ready to receive the -didBeginContact: method call from the physics world. Let's implement that method:

07-MorePhysics/step05/PhysicsBall/RCWMyScene.m

```
- (void)didBeginContact:(SKPhysicsContact *)contact
{
    NSLog(@"In -didBeginContact:");
    NSLog(@"bodyA: %@", contact.bodyA);
    NSLog(@"bodyB: %@", contact.bodyB);
}
```

This method is called by the physics world to tell us when two physics bodies come into contact with each other. The SKPhysicsContact parameter gives useful information that you can learn about the contact, such as fetching the first and second bodies through the bodyA and bodyB properties, respectively. For the moment, we're just printing the description of these bodies to the console in Xcode so we can observe what happens as we go.

If you were to play the game right now, you would see nothing printed in the console yet. That's because we need to set an appropriate *bitmask* to categorize the bodies we want to watch for collisions.

To illustrate how bitmasks work, let's make two small changes. First, we'll add this line to the bumper constructor in the RCWBumperNode.m file.

07-MorePhysics/step05/PhysicsBall/RCWBumperNode.m

```
bumper.physicsBody = [SKPhysicsBody bodyWithRectangleOfSize:size];
➤ bumper.physicsBody.contactTestBitMask = 1;
```

The contactTestBitMask property is how we flag this physics body so that the physics world knows what kind of bodies we want to be notified about when the ball collides with them. In this case, we are saying that we want to know about all bodies with the category 1. That number will become more clear shortly.

Next, in the RCWPinballNode.m file, let's add this line to the constructor method after creating the ball physics body.

```
07-MorePhysics/step05/PhysicsBall/RCWPinballNode.m
RCWPinballNode *node = [self spriteNodeWithImageNamed:@"pinball.png"];
node.size = CGSizeMake(sideSize, sideSize);
node.physicsBody = [SKPhysicsBody bodyWithCircleOfRadius:sideSize/2];
➤ node.physicsBody.categoryBitMask = 1;
// ...
```

The categoryBitMask property is our way of telling the physics world what categories this body belongs to. Here we are saying that the physics body representing the ball should have a category of 1. Combined with the contactTest-BitMask on the bumper's physics body, this tells the physics world to let us know every time the ball comes into contact with the bumper.

When we build and run the game now, we'll see a flurry of activity in the log console of Xcode as the ball bounces into bumpers. Our log statements are telling us every time a contact begins.

But also note how we are not told about the ball colliding with anything else in the scene. This is the power of the physics body category bitmasks. We can choose what kinds of collisions we need to be told about and just let the physics engine handle the rest on its own if we don't care.

A Quick Overview of Bitmasks

Bitmasks are a special computer science-y way to pack a lot of information into one property. The categoryBitMask property on the SKPhysicsBody objects is of type uint32_t, a 32-bit integer. In our experiment, we assigned the integer 1 to this property. But because we want each bit in the mask to represent a category, we need different integers to pick them:

```
00000000000000000000000000000000  is the integer 0 (no category)
00000000000000000000000000000001  is the integer 1 (category 1)
00000000000000000000000000000010  is the integer 2 (category 2)
00000000000000000000000000000100  is the integer 4 (category 3)
00000000000000000000000000001000  is the integer 8 (category 4)
... and so on
```

When a bit is on, or set to 1, that tells the physics world what category the body belongs to. The world then uses a *bitwise and* operation with the other bodies' contactTestBitMask values. If two bodies touch and the same bits in one body's category are turned on in the other body's contact-test bitmask, then the physics world knows that we want to be told about that contact.

Manually specifying integer values for bitmasks is a pain, though. That's where we will use a special enumerated type to name specific bits. Let's create a new RCWCategoriesMask.h file with these contents:

07-MorePhysics/step06/PhysicsBall/RCWCategoriesMask.h
```
typedef NS_OPTIONS(uint32_t, RCWCollisionCategory) {
    RCWCategoryBall       = 1 << 0,
    RCWCategoryBumper     = 1 << 1,
    RCWCategoryTarget     = 1 << 2,
};
```

Remember back when we used enumerated types for the left and right paddles in *Building Paddles with Bodies, Pins, and Torque*, on page 127? We didn't care what values the compiler assigned for us; we just wanted it to make up distinct values and name them so we could use them. Here, we want the compiler to use specific values for each of these constants, and we want the type of each to be uint32_t. NS_OPTIONS is similar to NS_ENUM in effect, but it gives the compiler the hint that this list of constants is part of a bitmask and not just a list of plain old integers.

That strange syntax for the RCWCategoryBall constant, the 1 << 0, is our way of telling the compiler that we want this number to start as the integer 1, which means that only the first bit is set, and then we want it to *bit shift* that bit to the left by zero spaces. In this case that means nothing happens, and we could leave the << 0 off and it would remain just "1". But it introduces you to the pattern and is essential to the next constant, RCWCategoryBumper, which shifts the bit over by one space, giving us the integer 2. We follow the pattern again for the RCWCategoryTarget constant. We could continue this pattern to build more categories, up to 32, and each constant would represent one bit in the bitmask.

To use this for the pinball game, let's import this header file at the top of the RCWPinballNode.h file.

07-MorePhysics/step06/PhysicsBall/RCWPinballNode.m
```
 #import "RCWPinballNode.h"
➤ #import "RCWCategoriesMask.h"
```

And then we'll set the category of the ball.

07-MorePhysics/step06/PhysicsBall/RCWPinballNode.m
```
 node.physicsBody = [SKPhysicsBody bodyWithCircleOfRadius:sideSize/2];
➤ node.physicsBody.categoryBitMask = RCWCategoryBall;
```

By assigning the RCWCategoryBall constant to the categoryBitMask, we are signaling to the physics world what category bit belongs to this body.

Now, let's switch to the RCWBumperNode.m file and import the same RCWCategories-Mask.h header file.

07-MorePhysics/step06/PhysicsBall/RCWBumperNode.m
```
#import "RCWBumperNode.h"
➤ #import "RCWCategoriesMask.h"
```

In the +bumperWithSize: method, we'll set up the category information on the physics body.

07-MorePhysics/step06/PhysicsBall/RCWBumperNode.m
```
bumper.physicsBody = [SKPhysicsBody bodyWithRectangleOfSize:size];
➤ bumper.physicsBody.categoryBitMask = RCWCategoryBumper;
➤ bumper.physicsBody.contactTestBitMask = RCWCategoryBall;
```

Instead of hard-coding an integer value, we are setting the category bitmask to the appropriate constant representing the bit for the bumper. Instead of hard-coding the ball's body for the contact-test bitmask, we're using the constant for that bit. Let's do the same thing for the target. We'll import the RCWCategoriesMask.h header file at the top of RCWTargetNode.m.

07-MorePhysics/step06/PhysicsBall/RCWTargetNode.m
```
#import "RCWTargetNode.h"
➤ #import "RCWCategoriesMask.h"
```

And then we'll assign the proper category constant in the +targetWithRadius: method, like we did with the bumper.

07-MorePhysics/step06/PhysicsBall/RCWTargetNode.m
```
target.physicsBody = [SKPhysicsBody bodyWithCircleOfRadius:radius];
➤ target.physicsBody.categoryBitMask = RCWCategoryTarget;
➤ target.physicsBody.contactTestBitMask = RCWCategoryBall;
```

All this activity to set up bitmask constants may seem like overkill for such a simple example, but it's a critical organizational skill as the physics simulations in your games grow in complexity. We now have a clear way to categorize bodies and test for collisions between only what we care about.

To recap, we set the categoryBitMask property to the bit that categorizes a particular physics body. Then we set the contactTestBitMask to mark which categories we care about. Then the physics world takes over and only notifies us in the -didBeginContact: method for the categories that pass the contact test and whose bits are set to 1.

Responding to Collisions

Great, so we get notified every time the ball collides with targets and bumpers. But how do we tell them apart? We want to do special animations and sound effects for both kinds of bodies, but we only want to increase the user's score when the ball hits a target.

Let's go back and revisit the current state of the -didBeginContact: method in the RCWMyScene.m file.

```
07-MorePhysics/step05/PhysicsBall/RCWMyScene.m
- (void)didBeginContact:(SKPhysicsContact *)contact
{
    NSLog(@"In -didBeginContact:");
    NSLog(@"bodyA: %@", contact.bodyA);
    NSLog(@"bodyB: %@", contact.bodyB);
}
```

When two bodies contact each other, how do we know which one is bodyA and which one is bodyB? Unfortunately, we don't know, and Apple explicitly says that we should check *both* bodies to see which one of them is the ball.

To tell the difference, we'll introduce an if statement to check the category on both bodies and then call a separate method once we know for sure.

```
07-MorePhysics/step07/PhysicsBall/RCWMyScene.m
- (void)didBeginContact:(SKPhysicsContact *)contact
{
    if (contact.bodyA.categoryBitMask == RCWCategoryBall) {
        [self ballBody:contact.bodyA didContact:contact withBody:contact.bodyB];
    } else if (contact.bodyB.categoryBitMask == RCWCategoryBall) {
        [self ballBody:contact.bodyB didContact:contact withBody:contact.bodyA];
    }
}
```

Here we are checking to see whether the categoryBitMask of bodyA is the same as the RCWCategoryBall. If it is, then we call a new method, ballPhysicsBody:didContact-PhysicsBody:, with bodyA, which we know for a fact is the ball. If bodyB's category bitmask matches the ball, then we call the same method with bodyB as the first parameter instead.

The scene doesn't know about these category constants until we import the RCWCategoriesMask.h header, so let's do that now.

```
07-MorePhysics/step07/PhysicsBall/RCWMyScene.m
#import "RCWMyScene.h"
#import "RCWPinballNode.h"
#import "RCWPlungerNode.h"
#import "RCWTableNode.h"
#import "RCWPaddleNode.h"
#import "RCWHUDNode.h"
➤ #import "RCWCategoriesMask.h"
➤ #import "RCWTargetNode.h"
```

Now let's write the -ballBody:didContact:withBody: method to play sounds and add points to the score.

07-MorePhysics/step07/PhysicsBall/RCWMyScene.m

```objc
- (void)ballBody:(SKPhysicsBody *)ballBody
      didContact:(SKPhysicsContact *)contact
        withBody:(SKPhysicsBody *)otherBody
{
    if (otherBody.categoryBitMask == RCWCategoryBumper) {
        [self playRandomBumperSound];
    } else if (otherBody.categoryBitMask == RCWCategoryTarget) {
        [self playRandomTargetSound];
        RCWTargetNode *target = (RCWTargetNode *)otherBody.node;
        [self addPoints:target.pointValue];
    }
}
```

By the time this method is run, there's no ambiguity. We know exactly which physics body is the ball. We just need to figure out what that other body is and act on it. That's where the categoryBitMask comes in handy again. Because we have only a handful of categories and they don't overlap, we are comparing the category bitmask value of the other body directly to the RCWCategoryBumper and RCWCategoryTarget constants, respectively.

For the bumpers, we just play a random bumper sound. For the target, we play a random target sound but also find the target node and pass its pointValue to a method we'll write to add points to the player's score. Remember that we set this pointValue property when we loaded the targets into the table from the property list configuration file back in *Loading Targets and Bumpers from a Layout File*, on page 136.

Let's write the two sound-playing methods.

07-MorePhysics/step07/PhysicsBall/RCWMyScene.m

```objc
- (void)playRandomBumperSound
{
    NSInteger soundCount = [self.bumperSounds count];
    NSInteger randomSoundIndex = arc4random_uniform((u_int32_t)soundCount);
    SKAction *sound = self.bumperSounds[randomSoundIndex];
    [self runAction:sound];
}

- (void)playRandomTargetSound
{
    NSInteger soundCount = [self.targetSounds count];
    NSInteger randomSoundIndex = arc4random_uniform((u_int32_t)soundCount);
    SKAction *sound = self.targetSounds[randomSoundIndex];
    [self runAction:sound];
}
```

We're using a fun auditory trick to delight the player and randomly picking from similar sets of sounds for the bumper and target. In this case we have two array properties: self.bumperSounds and self.targetSounds. Each of these methods respectively picks a random sound action from these arrays and runs it on the scene. The effect gives a more natural feel to the game because the same hit doesn't necessarily sound the same way every time.

We need to add those two array properties to the class extension at the top of the file.

07-MorePhysics/step07/PhysicsBall/RCWMyScene.m
```
@interface RCWMyScene ()
<SKPhysicsContactDelegate>
@property (nonatomic, weak) UITouch *plungerTouch;
@property (nonatomic, weak) UITouch *leftPaddleTouch;
@property (nonatomic, weak) UITouch *rightPaddleTouch;

➤ @property (nonatomic, strong) NSArray *bumperSounds;
➤ @property (nonatomic, strong) NSArray *targetSounds;
@end
```

And then we need to initialize them at the end of the -setUpScene method.

07-MorePhysics/step07/PhysicsBall/RCWMyScene.m
```
self.bumperSounds = @[
    [SKAction playSoundFileNamed:@"bump1.aif" waitForCompletion:NO],
    [SKAction playSoundFileNamed:@"bump2.aif" waitForCompletion:NO],
    [SKAction playSoundFileNamed:@"bump3.aif" waitForCompletion:NO]];
self.targetSounds = @[
    [SKAction playSoundFileNamed:@"target1.aif" waitForCompletion:NO],
    [SKAction playSoundFileNamed:@"target2.aif" waitForCompletion:NO],
    [SKAction playSoundFileNamed:@"target3.aif" waitForCompletion:NO]];
```

Each property holds an array of sound actions with slightly different sounds from the app bundle. The two sound methods pick random sounds to play from these arrays every time. Let's grab the files themselves from the 07-More-Physics/step07 directory of the book's sample code.

Next, we'll implement the -addPoints: method to find the RCWHUDNode and increase the score.

07-MorePhysics/step07/PhysicsBall/RCWMyScene.m
```
- (void)addPoints:(NSUInteger)points
{
    RCWHUDNode *hud = (RCWHUDNode *)[self childNodeWithName:@"hud"];
    [hud addPoints:points];
}
```

We find the node by name and then call its -addPoints: method to update the display.

Go ahead and play the game for a bit and enjoy!

We've walked through the basics of taking the SKPhysicsContact object given to us in the -didBeginContact: method and making sounds depending on what the ball collided with. We figured out which contact body was which and then played the appropriate sounds and animations.

But we're not finished with collision detection yet. We need to make some minor adjustments to the ball's velocity to make sure it doesn't continue to accelerate out of control as it runs into bumpers and targets.

Slowing Down the Ball on Rebound

You've surely noticed that as the ball bounces back and forth between the obstacles, it quickly zooms out of control. The high restitution values on the bumpers and targets increase the speed of the ball with every hit. As the ball ricochets around long enough, it picks up speed that even the best human couldn't handle. We want the restitution to increase the speed of the ball, but we want to cap the ball's rebound speed to keep the game playable.

More trigonometry to the rescue! Let's write a method named capPhysics-Body:atSpeed: that we can call to slow down any physics body we want in the scene.

07-MorePhysics/step08/PhysicsBall/RCWMyScene.m
```
- (void)capPhysicsBody:(SKPhysicsBody *)body atSpeed:(CGFloat)maxSpeed
{
    CGFloat speed = sqrt(pow(body.velocity.dx, 2) +
                         pow(body.velocity.dy, 2));

    if (speed > maxSpeed) {
        speed = maxSpeed;
        CGFloat angle = atan2(body.velocity.dy, body.velocity.dx);
        CGVector limitedVelocity = CGVectorMake(speed*cos(angle), speed*sin(angle));
        body.velocity = limitedVelocity;
    }
}
```

We find the current speed of the body by calculating the hypotenuse of the right triangle made up of the body's x and y velocity components. If we see that the speed is greater than the maxSpeed, we compose a capped velocity and assign it to the body. No matter how fast the body was going to go after the rebound, its velocity will be limited to this speed before the physics engine runs calculations for the next frame.

Let's tweak the ballBody:didContact:withBody: method to call this method to cap the speed of the ball.

07-MorePhysics/step08/PhysicsBall/RCWMyScene.m

```
- (void)ballBody:(SKPhysicsBody *)ballBody
     didContact:(SKPhysicsContact *)contact
       withBody:(SKPhysicsBody *)otherBody
{
    if (otherBody.categoryBitMask == RCWCategoryBumper) {
        [self playRandomBumperSound];
    } else if (otherBody.categoryBitMask == RCWCategoryTarget) {
        [self playRandomTargetSound];
        RCWTargetNode *target = (RCWTargetNode *)otherBody.node;
        [self addPoints:target.pointValue];
    }

    if (otherBody.categoryBitMask & (RCWCategoryBumper | RCWCategoryTarget)) {
        [self capPhysicsBody:ballBody atSpeed:1150];
    }

}
```

We need to call this new capPhysicsBody:atSpeed: method for *both* the target and bumper collisions. Although we could repeat this method call twice in each conditional clause we already had, adding this new conditional clause illustrates how powerful the category bitmasks can be.

We are saying that if the otherBody category is either a bumper or a target, then call the capPhysicsBody:atSpeed: method. The logical-or (|) operator combines the bits of the RCWCategoryBumper and RCWCategoryTarget constants together, and the logical-and (&) operator *tests* to see whether both bits are set in the otherBody.categoryBitMask property.

This lets us mix and match any combination of bits in our bitmask to represent the different categories of bodies and how they interact. In this case, we have some behaviors we want to exhibit on contact with either the target or the bumper, and we have some behaviors we want to exhibit on contact with both. Check out Wikipedia for more information about logical operations and bitmasks.[3]

Let's use this moment to add another behavior when either a target or a bumper is hit. We'll add a method on the scene that takes a node and runs some animation actions to make it briefly flash a red color.

---

3. http://en.wikipedia.org/wiki/Bitmask

07-MorePhysics/step08/PhysicsBall/RCWMyScene.m
```
- (void)flashNode:(SKNode *)node
{
    SKAction *scaleUp = [SKAction scaleTo:1.1 duration:0.05];
    SKAction *scaleDown = [SKAction scaleTo:1 duration:0.1];
    SKAction *colorize = [SKAction colorizeWithColor:[SKColor redColor]
                                      colorBlendFactor:200
                                              duration:0];
    SKAction *uncolorize = [SKAction colorizeWithColorBlendFactor:0 duration:0];

    SKAction *all = [SKAction sequence:@[colorize, scaleUp, scaleDown, uncolorize]];

    [node runAction:all];
}
```

Running a sequence of actions on a node is a familiar process that you learned back in Chapter 2, *Actions: Go, Sprite, Go!*, on page 13, but here we meet a couple of new actions: -colorizeWithColor:colorBlendFactor:duration: and -colorizeWithColorBlendFactor:duration. Those two actions let us make a red tint fade overtop of the node and then fade away. Combined with the quick scale-up and scale-down effect, it gives the impression that the node got bumped.

Now let's change the ballBody:didContact:withBody: method to also flash bumpers and targets.

07-MorePhysics/step08/PhysicsBall/RCWMyScene.m
```
if (otherBody.categoryBitMask & (RCWCategoryBumper | RCWCategoryTarget)) {
    [self capPhysicsBody:ballBody atSpeed:1150];
➤    [self flashNode:otherBody.node];
}
```

Wonderful! As the ball hits the bumpers and targets, it can't rebound too fast. And when it hits bumpers and targets, they quickly flash to add to the fun visual frenzy on the screen.

Phew! That's a lot to wade through. Although it's easy to start with, the physics engine is marvelously rich and complex. We've only scratched the surface. We'll be touching more on physics in the next chapter as we polish up the pinball game, but we still won't cover all the possibilities. Check out Apple's adventure game sample code for another excellent example.[4]

Our pinball game is quite functional at this point, but we can put more polish on it while leveraging more goodies in the Sprite Kit toolbox. Let's tackle that next.

---

4. https://developer.apple.com/library/ios/documentation/GraphicsAnimation/Conceptual/CodeExplainedAdventure/AdventureArchitecture/AdventureArchitecture.html

Polishing the Pinball Game

The pinball game works great so far, but we're not quite finished yet. We're going to use a few more deep Sprite Kit tricks to polish it up. We'll build an animated cue for the player when the game begins and the plunger is ready to be pulled. We'll add a new target that gives a 3X score bonus while it spins. We'll show puffs of smoke every time the ball bounces off a target or bumper. And we'll cover the pinball table with a partially transparent node to give the scene texture and depth.

By the end of this eclectic set of steps, you'll have even more understanding of the deeper parts of Sprite Kit, such as non-colliding body contact, frame-based sprite animations, texture atlases, and fixing the game so it stays in portrait orientation.

Ready? Let's go!

Cueing the Player to Pull the Plunger with Sprite Animations

When the game begins, the ball comes to rest on the plunger but nothing else happens. What kind of cue can we give to the player on how to launch it? For this example, we're going to play an animated series of triangles moving down over the ball (think of a marquee) that gives a visual hint of what to do. See Figure 35, *Frame-based animation cue to pull the plunger down*, on page 156 for an example of each of the frames.

To implement this, you must learn about frame-based animations and texture atlases. Each image of the marching triangles will exist as an individual texture that we play in sequence on a sprite node with a special SKAction. Because we don't want to get bogged down in details we've already covered about adding image assets and managing the Xcode project, we're going to start with the

Frame: 1 2 3 4 5

Figure 35—Frame-based animation cue to pull the plunger down

code as it is in the 08-Polish/step01 directory of the sample code that accompanies the book. Refer back to *Preface*, on page vii, if you don't have it yet.

Playing Frames of Animation in a Sprite Node

As we've done throughout the pinball game, we're going to create a custom SKNode subclass for our animation node that knows how to set itself up and gives us a simple pair of methods to activate and deactivate it.

Let's create a new file in Xcode named RCWPullHintNode.h with these contents for the header:

08-Polish/step02/PhysicsBall/RCWPullHintNode.h

```
#import <SpriteKit/SpriteKit.h>

@interface RCWPullHintNode : SKNode
+ (instancetype)pullHint;
- (void)showHint;
- (void)hideHint;
@end
```

We have the constructor method and two utility methods we will call to show and hide the hint animation. Now let's create the corresponding implementation file, RCWPullHintNode.m, and start building the constructor implementation.

08-Polish/step02/PhysicsBall/RCWPullHintNode.m

```
#import "RCWPullHintNode.h"
@implementation RCWPullHintNode
+ (instancetype)pullHint
{
    RCWPullHintNode *hint = [self node];
    SKSpriteNode *animation = [SKSpriteNode node];
    animation.name = @"animation";
```

```
    [hint addChild:animation];
    animation.size = CGSizeMake(12, 62);

    // ...

    return hint;
}
@end
```

In the +pullHint method, we first construct an empty node with the +node method on this subclass. Then we construct a child sprite node that will actually hold the animation. We're using a child node here because that gives us more flexibility to animate its position with actions relative to the parent node's fixed position on the table. This is similar to why we built a container node to make it easy to position the visible part of the plunger as it moves in *Using Node Subclasses to Separate Responsibility,* on page 107.

Notice how the animation sprite node is constructed with the +node method and not the usual +spriteNodeWithImageNamed: method. That's because we don't need it to start off with an image. Instead, we want to immediately play a series of textures on this node as an animation. We'll add this code to the constructor next, just above the return statement.

08-Polish/step02/PhysicsBall/RCWPullHintNode.m
```
➤ NSArray *frames = @[[SKTexture textureWithImageNamed:@"pull-hint-0"],
➤                     [SKTexture textureWithImageNamed:@"pull-hint-1"],
➤                     [SKTexture textureWithImageNamed:@"pull-hint-2"],
➤                     [SKTexture textureWithImageNamed:@"pull-hint-3"],
➤                     [SKTexture textureWithImageNamed:@"pull-hint-4"]];
➤ SKAction *play = [SKAction animateWithTextures:frames timePerFrame:0.2];
➤ SKAction *playForever = [SKAction repeatActionForever:play];
➤ [animation runAction:playForever];
```

```
    return hint;
```

Here we meet SKTexture for the first time. Every time we create a sprite node, we're using SKTexture objects under the hood, but they're hidden away from us by the simple interface with the sprite nodes. In this case, we need to load the textures directly to create an array of them. We then take that array of frames and pass them to the +animateWithTextures:timePerFrame: action to play them back with 0.2 seconds between each frame. We pass that action to the +repeatActionForever: method to get a repeating action and then run the final action on the animation node.

The net effect is that this node contains an animation that constantly flips through all the textures to give the illusion that we have an animated marquee of triangles.

We need to fade this effect in on cue, so next let's start building the -showHint method.

08-Polish/step02/PhysicsBall/RCWPullHintNode.m

```
- (void)showHint
{
    if (self.alpha == 1 || [self actionForKey:@"showAction"]) {
        return;
    }
    [self removeActionForKey:@"hideAction"];

    // ...

}
```

We first use some conditional guard clauses to make this method more robust. If we call this method more than once while the animation is showing, it will just return and ignore the request since there's nothing to do. We are checking for two situations: if the alpha is 1, then we are already visible. Or, if there is an action with the key showAction, then we're in the process of showing the node. In either case, the method should not continue.

Once we get past the guard statement, we immediately remove any action that might have been run with the key hideAction. As you can probably guess, we're using this key for the action that does the reverse of this method's work. If the hide action was already running, we want to stop it so that we can run the show action instead. Refer back to *Powering Down After a Few Seconds*, on page 35, for a refresher on how action keys work.

Next we finish the method by running all the actions that make the sprite node fade and swoop in to cue the player.

08-Polish/step02/PhysicsBall/RCWPullHintNode.m

```
- (void)showHint
{
    if (self.alpha == 1 || [self actionForKey:@"showAction"]) {
        return;
    }
    [self removeActionForKey:@"hideAction"];

➤   SKAction *fadeIn = [SKAction fadeAlphaTo:1 duration:0.6];
➤   SKAction *slide = [SKAction moveToY:0 duration:0.2];
➤   SKAction *slideChild = [SKAction runAction:slide onChildWithName:@"animation"];
➤   SKAction *zoom = [SKAction scaleTo:1 duration:0.2];
➤   SKAction *zoomChild = [SKAction runAction:zoom onChildWithName:@"animation"];
➤
➤   SKAction *showAction = [SKAction group:@[slideChild, zoomChild, fadeIn]];
➤   [self runAction:showAction withKey:@"showAction"];
}
```

The fadeIn action runs on this RCWPullHintNode instance, but notice how the slide and zoom actions are run on the child node. We build two new actions, slideChild and zoomChild, that perform the actions on child nodes with specific names, even though they are run on the parent node. While we could run these actions on the child node directly, using the +runAction:onChildWithName: action lets us group all these related actions together under one key so we can cancel the whole lot without trying to look them up individually.

We build the showAction group that slides, zooms, and fades all at once. Finally, we run the action on the RCWPullHintNode object with the key showAction.

Now, let's build the sister method to hide the hint.

08-Polish/step02/PhysicsBall/RCWPullHintNode.m
```
- (void)hideHint
{
    if (self.alpha == 0 || [self actionForKey:@"hideAction"]) {
        return;
    }
    [self removeActionForKey:@"showAction"];
    SKAction *fadeOut = [SKAction fadeAlphaTo:0 duration:0.1];
    SKAction *slide = [SKAction moveToY:30 duration:0.2];
    SKAction *slideChild = [SKAction runAction:slide onChildWithName:@"animation"];
    SKAction *zoom = [SKAction scaleTo:1.3 duration:0.2];
    SKAction *zoomChild = [SKAction runAction:zoom onChildWithName:@"animation"];
    SKAction *hideAction = [SKAction group:@[fadeOut, slideChild, zoomChild]];
    [self runAction:hideAction withKey:@"hideAction"];
}
```

This just reverses what we did in the -showHint method. We first check to see whether we're already hidden or in the process of hiding. Then we remove the show action if it is already running so we can take over. Then we build the fadeout, slide, and zoom to get the effect we want and run the action on this node with the key hideAction.

We end up with two methods that undo each other. Time to put them to use. Let's switch over to the RCWMyScene.m file and add the header import at the top of the file so we can use it in the scene.

08-Polish/step02/PhysicsBall/RCWMyScene.m
```
#import "RCWMyScene.h"
#import "RCWPinballNode.h"
#import "RCWPlungerNode.h"
#import "RCWTableNode.h"
#import "RCWPaddleNode.h"
#import "RCWHUDNode.h"
#import "RCWCategoriesMask.h"
#import "RCWTargetNode.h"
➤ #import "RCWPullHintNode.h"
```

Then, in the -setUpScene method, right after we create the plunger, we'll create and position this pull hint and immediately hide it.

08-Polish/step02/PhysicsBall/RCWMyScene.m

```
// ...

RCWPlungerNode *plunger = [RCWPlungerNode plunger];
plunger.name = @"plunger";
plunger.position = CGPointMake(self.size.width - plunger.size.width/2 - 4,
                              plunger.size.height / 2);
[table addChild:plunger];

➤ RCWPullHintNode *pullHint = [RCWPullHintNode pullHint];
➤ pullHint.name = @"pullHint";
➤ pullHint.position = CGPointMake(plunger.position.x,
➤                                 plunger.position.y + plunger.size.height + 30);
➤ [pullHint hideHint];
➤ [table addChild:pullHint];

// ...
```

We place the hint just above the plunger so the player knows what the animation is meant for, name the node so we can find it later, tell it to hide itself, and then add it to the table.

To use this during gameplay, we'll change the -update: method to continually check to see whether the plunger is in contact with the ball.

08-Polish/step02/PhysicsBall/RCWMyScene.m

```
  - (void)update:(NSTimeInterval)currentTime
  {
➤     RCWPinballNode *ball = (id)[self childNodeWithName:@"//ball"];
➤     RCWPlungerNode *plunger = (id)[self childNodeWithName:@"//plunger"];
➤     RCWPullHintNode *hint = (id)[self childNodeWithName:@"//pullHint"];
➤     if ([plunger isInContactWithBall:ball]) {
➤         [hint showHint];
➤     } else {
➤         [hint hideHint];
➤     }

      if (self.leftPaddleTouch) {
          RCWPaddleNode *leftPaddle = (id)[self childNodeWithName:@"//leftPaddle"];
          [leftPaddle flip];
      }

      if (self.rightPaddleTouch) {
          RCWPaddleNode *rightPaddle = (id)[self childNodeWithName:@"//rightPaddle"];
          [rightPaddle flip];
      }
  }
```

We look up the ball, the plunger, and the hint node. If the -isInContactWithBall: method on the plunger returns true, then we call -showHint on the hint node. Otherwise, we call -hideHint. Notice that this means we are calling these methods over and over every frame while we check to see whether the ball is resting on the plunger. That's why we wrote the hint methods to check to see whether their work had already been completed. This makes them very fast, and we can call them over and over again without worrying about performance at this point.

That's all it takes for the animation! Run the game now, and you'll see the triangle marquee fade and swoop into view whenever the ball comes to rest on the plunger.

Moving Textures into a Texture Atlas for Great Performance

Now that you've been introduced to the idea of SKTexture objects, it's time to briefly talk about texture atlases. The games we are working on in this book are quite simple. There are very few graphics and relatively few nodes at work in the scene. But as your games get more complex, your graphics demands will put increasing pressure on the GPU of these remarkably small devices. Indeed, most of the processing power used up by your game could be from Sprite Kit loading and shoving pixels around on the screen.

That's where texture atlases come in. The way we've been building these games so far, we've added separate PNG files for each image texture to the Xcode project. Because they are part of the game target, they are automatically optimized and copied into the app bundle on build. We don't have to do anything special to use them in an SKSpriteNode or an SKTexture instance. We just need to refer to them by filename.

But loading these files takes time. And, by default, each file takes up a separate OpenGL texture in the GPU memory. While fast for these simple games, it is very slow for a game with a lot of frame-based animations. It's common for 2D games to have thousands of individual textures that are referenced throughout the sprites on the screen.

What we want is a way to combine individual image files into a single *texture atlas* that is efficiently reused by OpenGL under the hood. When finally compiled, a texture atlas looks like Figure 36, *Texture atlas of pinball sprites*, on page 162.

Everything is rotated and positioned to get the sprites as tightly packed as possible. This single texture is then loaded in the GPU, and when you want

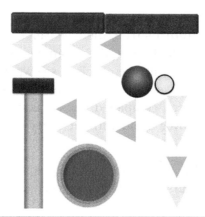

Figure 36—Texture atlas of pinball sprites

to use a specific slice out of this atlas, you specify boundaries and rotation of the one you want.

In most other game frameworks, you have to build these texture atlases yourself with a separate process or build tool. But Sprite Kit, in combination with Xcode, does all the work for you automatically! You don't even have to change your existing code to make it work. All you have to do is put your images in a special .atlas directory in the project, as in the following figure.

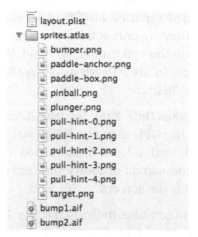

Figure 37—Images files in an .atlas directory

Take a look at the Xcode project in the 08-Polish/step03 directory of the sample code that came with this book. You'll see a sprites.atlas directory with all the game sprites inside of it. If you name a directory with the extension .atlas and drag it into the Xcode sidebar, then Xcode will automatically compile any images in that directory for you, even if you add more later. You don't have to do anything else!

The SKSpriteNode and SKTexture classes will check first for a reference in a texture atlas that matches the original filename. If it sees what you want in an atlas, it will automatically use it. Otherwise, it will fall back to looking for a stand-alone image file in your bundle.

This is a powerful feature made incredibly easy by Sprite Kit's API and integration with Xcode. It's tough to beat. Find out more by reading Apple's documentation.[1]

Next up, let's use physics contact detection to build a special target that the ball passes through to turn on bonus scoring!

Adding Bonus Points with a Spinner

Bumpers and bouncy targets are fun, but we'd like to add another kind of element to the pinball table for the player. We're going to build a spinner that is activated when the ball passes through it. While the spinner is rotating, targets are worth three times their normal point value—it's a bonus mode! As the spinner slows to a stop, the bonus mode deactivates. If the player can keep the spinner in motion, the points will just keep piling up.

To do this we'll need to build a new node subclass and lay it out on the table in the property list configuration file we set up back in *Loading Targets and Bumpers from a Layout File*, on page 136. We'll also use a new technique when detecting body contact with the physics engine. Bodies don't have to be solid. We're going to allow the ball to pass through the spinner node yet still detect the collision so we can give it a spin.

First, we'll create a new file in the Xcode project named RCWBonusSpinnerNode.h to hold the class header.

```
08-Polish/step04/PhysicsBall/RCWBonusSpinnerNode.h
#import <SpriteKit/SpriteKit.h>

@interface RCWBonusSpinnerNode : SKSpriteNode
+ (instancetype)bonusSpinnerNode;
- (void)spin;
@property (nonatomic, readonly) BOOL stillSpinning;
@end
```

---

1. https://developer.apple.com/library/ios/recipes/xcode_help-texture_atlas/AboutTextureAtlases/AboutTextureAtlases.html

We're going to implement a constructor method, build an instance method to tell it to spin, and use a read-only property to find out whether the node is still spinning. Remember that we're doing our best to build nodes as self-contained black boxes with well-defined APIs.

Let's create a file named RCWBonusSpinnerNode.m and start it with the constructor implementation.

```
08-Polish/step04/PhysicsBall/RCWBonusSpinnerNode.m
#import "RCWBonusSpinnerNode.h"
#import "RCWCategoriesMask.h"
@implementation RCWBonusSpinnerNode
+ (instancetype)bonusSpinnerNode
{
    RCWBonusSpinnerNode *spinner = [self spriteNodeWithImageNamed:@"bonus-spinner"];
    spinner.size = CGSizeMake(6, 40);
    spinner.physicsBody = [SKPhysicsBody bodyWithRectangleOfSize:spinner.size];
    spinner.physicsBody.affectedByGravity = NO;
    spinner.physicsBody.angularDamping = 0.8;
    spinner.physicsBody.categoryBitMask = RCWCategoryBonusSpinner;
    spinner.physicsBody.contactTestBitMask = RCWCategoryBall;
    spinner.physicsBody.collisionBitMask = 0;
    return spinner;
}
@end
```

We first create a RCWBonusSpinnerNode as a sprite node with the image named bonus-spinner.png and size it so it looks nice. Then we set up the physics body to ignore gravity and set the angularDamping property to 0.8 to cause the body to slow down quickly when it spins. We give it a new category in the category-BitMask property and set the contactTestBitMask property so that the physics world knows we want to be told when it comes in contact with the ball. For a refresher on all of this, refer back to Chapter 7, *More Physics: Paddles and Collisions*, on page 127.

Then things get interesting. We set the collisionBitMask property to zero, which is the cue to the physics world that we don't want the physics engine to make this body appear solid to any other body category. Anything that comes in contact with this body should just pass through it.

The collisionBitMask property is a bitmask just the same as the contactTestBitMask property. The bits in that 32-bit integer are cues to the physics world about which bodies should appear solid to each other. By setting this property to zero, we are saying that this body should be a ghost. It will certainly participate in the collision detection, but we don't want the physics engine to act on it. We want to do special work with it instead.

We must add this new RCWCategoryBonusSpinner constant to the list of categories in RCWCategoriesMask.h so the compiler knows about the bit constant.

08-Polish/step04/PhysicsBall/RCWCategoriesMask.h
```
typedef NS_OPTIONS(uint32_t, RCWCollisionCategory) {
    RCWCategoryBall        = 1 << 0,
    RCWCategoryBumper      = 1 << 1,
    RCWCategoryTarget      = 1 << 2,
➤   RCWCategoryBonusSpinner = 1 << 3,
};
```

Notice how we're continuing the pattern we started before saying that the RCWCategoryBonusSpinner constant represents the fourth bit from the right of a 32-bit integer. We'd keep going if we had more categories to keep track of.

But we've set only one side of the equation. To truly make sure this body isn't a hard surface for the ball, we have to clear the bit on the ball's physics body for the bonus spinner. Switch to RCWPinballNode.m and add an extra line after setting up the categoryBitMask property.

08-Polish/step04/PhysicsBall/RCWPinballNode.m
```
node.physicsBody = [SKPhysicsBody bodyWithCircleOfRadius:sideSize/2];
node.physicsBody.categoryBitMask = RCWCategoryBall;
➤ node.physicsBody.collisionBitMask ^= RCWCategoryBonusSpinner;
// ...
```

That funny ^= syntax is how we tell the C compiler to toggle specific bit positions of the property and then reassign the result to the property. The ^ operator is called *bitwise exclusive-or*, which is just a fancy way of saying that we are flipping bits from what they used to be. Refer back to *Slowing Down the Ball on Rebound*, on page 152, for more discussion about these bitwise math operations.

By default, the collisionBitMask property has all bits turned on, or set to 1. By using this ^= operator, we are telling the compiler to turn off the category bit for the RCWCategoryBonusSpinner. Because we turned all the bits off for the spinner node's collisionBitMask property, and the spinner node category bit is off for the ball's collisionBitMask property, they will effectively pass through each other.

Because this spinner is a ghost in the scene, when the ball comes in contact we need to spin it manually. That's why we have to implement our own -spin method back in RCWBonusSpinnerNode.m.

08-Polish/step04/PhysicsBall/RCWBonusSpinnerNode.m
```
- (void)spin
{
    [self.physicsBody applyAngularImpulse:0.003];
}
```

All this does is reach into the physics body and apply a slight angular impulse. It's fast enough to cause this body to spin wildly. And it will slow down relatively quickly because of how we set the angularDamping in the constructor. We can adjust these values to taste.

Because we need to find out whether this node is spinning, we need to add the getter for the stillSpinning property.

08-Polish/step04/PhysicsBall/RCWBonusSpinnerNode.m
```
- (BOOL)stillSpinning
{
    return self.physicsBody.angularVelocity > 0.9;
}
```

We reach into the physics body and check to see whether the angularVelocity at this moment is greater than a certain threshold. Again, we can adjust these values to taste.

This node will be positioned using the property list configuration file, just like all of the other elements on the pinball table. Refer back to *Loading Targets and Bumpers from a Layout File*, on page 136, for more details about how we set that up. Because it's the table node's responsibility to read that file and load everything, we'll switch to RCWTableNode.m and add an import for the RCWBonusSpinnerNode.h header file at the top.

08-Polish/step04/PhysicsBall/RCWTableNode.m
```
#import "RCWTableNode.h"
#import "RCWBumperNode.h"
#import "RCWTargetNode.h"
➤ #import "RCWBonusSpinnerNode.h"
```

Then we'll add this bit of code to the end of the -loadLayoutNamed: to read configuration information from the dictionary that is pulled from the property list file.

08-Polish/step04/PhysicsBall/RCWTableNode.m
```
- (void)loadLayoutNamed:(NSString *)name
{
    // ...

    NSDictionary *spinnerConfig = layout[@"bonusSpinner"];
    RCWBonusSpinnerNode *spinner = [RCWBonusSpinnerNode bonusSpinnerNode];
    spinner.name = @"spinner";
    spinner.position = CGPointMake([spinnerConfig[@"x"] floatValue],
                                   [spinnerConfig[@"y"] floatValue]);
    [self addChild:spinner];
}
```

Similar to what we did with the targets and bumpers, we pull the spinner configuration from the bonusSpinner key in the layout dictionary. We set the spinner's name so we can find it later, and then set its position to the floating-point values in the configuration dictionary before adding it to the table. You can find the updated layout.plist file with the values for the bonusSpinner key in the 08-Polish/step04 directory of the book's sample code.

Let's switch to RCWMyScene.m and add an import for the RCWBonusSpinnerNode.h header file.

08-Polish/step04/PhysicsBall/RCWMyScene.m

```
#import "RCWMyScene.h"
#import "RCWPinballNode.h"
#import "RCWPlungerNode.h"
#import "RCWTableNode.h"
#import "RCWPaddleNode.h"
#import "RCWHUDNode.h"
#import "RCWCategoriesMask.h"
#import "RCWTargetNode.h"
#import "RCWPullHintNode.h"
➤ #import "RCWBonusSpinnerNode.h"
```

Then, in the -ballBody:didContact:withBody: method, we'll add the code to spin the spinner if the ball touches it.

08-Polish/step04/PhysicsBall/RCWMyScene.m

```
- (void)ballBody:(SKPhysicsBody *)ballBody
      didContact:(SKPhysicsContact *)contact
        withBody:(SKPhysicsBody *)otherBody
{
    if (otherBody.categoryBitMask == RCWCategoryBumper) {
        [self playRandomBumperSound];
    } else if (otherBody.categoryBitMask == RCWCategoryTarget) {
        [self playRandomTargetSound];
        RCWTargetNode *target = (RCWTargetNode *)otherBody.node;
        [self addPoints:target.pointValue];
    }

    if (otherBody.categoryBitMask & (RCWCategoryBumper | RCWCategoryTarget)) {
        [self capPhysicsBody:ballBody atSpeed:1150];
        [self flashNode:otherBody.node];
    }

➤   if (otherBody.categoryBitMask == RCWCategoryBonusSpinner) {
➤       RCWBonusSpinnerNode *spinner = (RCWBonusSpinnerNode *)otherBody.node;
➤       [spinner spin];
➤   }
}
```

If the body that the ball touches has the same category as the bonus spinner, then we can grab the node that the body belongs to and tell it to spin. All that's left to do is change the -addPoints: method so it multiplies points by three when the node is spinning.

08-Polish/step04/PhysicsBall/RCWMyScene.m

```
- (void)addPoints:(NSUInteger)points
{
    RCWHUDNode *hud = (RCWHUDNode *)[self childNodeWithName:@"hud"];
➤   RCWBonusSpinnerNode *spinner = (id)[self childNodeWithName:@"//spinner"];
➤   if (spinner.stillSpinning) {
➤       [hud addPoints:points * 3];
➤   } else {
➤       [hud addPoints:points];
➤   }
}
```

We look up the spinner node and check to see whether the stillSpinning property returns true. If so, then we tell the RCWHUDNode instance to add three times the points.

That's it! If players can skillfully maneuver the ball to pass through the spinner node, they'll be rewarded with a temporary boost in point value. Because the bonus mode is dependent on the spinning momentum of the physics body, and because the body naturally slows down, we don't have to do anything to turn if off. It's a bonus mode controlled entirely by the physics world!

Next up, we'll add some extra visual heft by showing puffs of smoke when the ball strikes targets and bumpers.

Showing Puffs of Smoke When Hitting Targets and Bumpers

The particle emitters we added to *Space Run* were so much fun that we just can't leave them out of our pinball game. We're going to add little puffs of smoke everywhere the ball hits a target or bumper, but to make it look more realistic we need to figure out the angle of that puff.

That's where the SKPhysicsContact object comes in. It exposes a contactPoint property that gives us the precise position of the collision between the two bodies in scene coordinates. Once we convert those coordinates into the table nodes coordinate system, then we can place quick particle emitters into the scene at that point. It also exposes the collisionImpulse property to tell us how hard the hit was. This gives us enough information to give the player the impression of speed!

We went in depth with particle emitters back in Chapter 3, *Explosions and Particle Effects*, on page 37—how to create them and how to load them. Here we're going to start with the Xcode project as it is in 08-Polish/step05 in the sample code for this chapter. That already has a small particle emitter and the helper category to load and play the emitter briefly in the scene. Starting at this point will keep us from getting distracted by details we've already covered.

Because we want to use our special SKEmitterNode category in the scene, we'll import the header file at the top of the RCWMyScene.m file.

08-Polish/step06/PhysicsBall/RCWMyScene.m
```
#import "RCWMyScene.h"
#import "RCWPinballNode.h"
#import "RCWPlungerNode.h"
#import "RCWTableNode.h"
#import "RCWPaddleNode.h"
#import "RCWHUDNode.h"
#import "RCWCategoriesMask.h"
#import "RCWTargetNode.h"
#import "RCWPullHintNode.h"
#import "RCWBonusSpinnerNode.h"
➤ #import "SKEmitterNode+RCWExtensions.h"
```

As we did with the explosion particle emitters in *Space Run*, we need to create a property that will hold a single particle emitter to use as a template and copy it when ready.

08-Polish/step06/PhysicsBall/RCWMyScene.m
```
@interface RCWMyScene ()
<SKPhysicsContactDelegate>
@property (nonatomic, weak) UITouch *plungerTouch;
@property (nonatomic, weak) UITouch *leftPaddleTouch;
@property (nonatomic, weak) UITouch *rightPaddleTouch;
@property (nonatomic, strong) NSArray *bumperSounds;
@property (nonatomic, strong) NSArray *targetSounds;
➤ @property (nonatomic, strong) SKEmitterNode *sparkTemplate;
@end
```

And we must initialize this template at the end of the -setUpScene method.

08-Polish/step06/PhysicsBall/RCWMyScene.m
```
self.targetSounds = @[
    [SKAction playSoundFileNamed:@"target1.aif" waitForCompletion:NO],
    [SKAction playSoundFileNamed:@"target2.aif" waitForCompletion:NO],
    [SKAction playSoundFileNamed:@"target3.aif" waitForCompletion:NO]];
➤ self.sparkTemplate = [SKEmitterNode rcw_nodeWithFile:@"Spark"];
```

Now we have an emitter node as a template that we'll be able to efficiently copy when we need it.

We want to display these puffs as the ball bounces into a bumper or a target. It just so happens that we already have a check for those categories of physics bodies in our -ballBody:didContact:withBody: method. Let's add a call to a method that will play the puff for that physics contact.

```
08-Polish/step06/PhysicsBall/RCWMyScene.m
- (void)ballBody:(SKPhysicsBody *)ballBody
        didContact:(SKPhysicsContact *)contact
          withBody:(SKPhysicsBody *)otherBody
{
    if (otherBody.categoryBitMask == RCWCategoryBumper) {
        [self playRandomBumperSound];
    } else if (otherBody.categoryBitMask == RCWCategoryTarget) {
        [self playRandomTargetSound];
        RCWTargetNode *target = (RCWTargetNode *)otherBody.node;
        [self addPoints:target.pointValue];
    }

    if (otherBody.categoryBitMask & (RCWCategoryBumper | RCWCategoryTarget)) {
        [self capPhysicsBody:ballBody atSpeed:1150];
        [self flashNode:otherBody.node];
        [self playPuffForContact:contact withVelocity:ballBody.velocity];
    }

    if (otherBody.categoryBitMask == RCWCategoryBonusSpinner) {
        RCWBonusSpinnerNode *spinner = (RCWBonusSpinnerNode *)otherBody.node;
        [spinner spin];
    }
}
```

As we set up back in *Slowing Down the Ball on Rebound*, on page 152, we already have the conditional check to see whether the body the ball bumped into is categorized as either RCWCategoryBumper or RCWCategoryTarget. We pass along the contact object and the ball's current velocity because we need to determine the angle at which to play the particle emitter.

Next, let's write the -playPuffForContact:withVelocity: method to do the work.

```
08-Polish/step06/PhysicsBall/RCWMyScene.m
- (void)playPuffForContact:(SKPhysicsContact *)contact
              withVelocity:(CGVector)velocity
{
    SKNode *table = [self childNodeWithName:@"table"];

    SKEmitterNode *spark = [self.sparkTemplate copy];

    spark.position = [self convertPoint:contact.contactPoint toNode:table];
```

```
    spark.xAcceleration = self.physicsWorld.gravity.dx;
    spark.yAcceleration = self.physicsWorld.gravity.dy;
    spark.emissionAngle = atan2(velocity.dy, velocity.dx);
    spark.particleSpeed = contact.collisionImpulse;

    [spark rcw_dieOutInDuration:0.05];

    [table addChild:spark];
}
```

We first look up the table node so we can compute the proper coordinates. We also create a copy of the spark node, which is much faster than loading it again from the app bundle. We set the spark's position to the contact.contactPoint after converting it to the coordinate system of the table node. We need to do the conversion because the table is larger than the scene. (Remember that we're using it to pan around and simulate a camera following the ball.)

After the spark is positioned, we alter some of the properties of the emitter node in real time to complete the illusion of the spark in response to the collision. The xAcceleration and yAcceleration properties are set to the physics world's current gravity. The emissionAngle is computed from the velocity of the ball using trigonometry with the atan2() function. That velocity is *after* the collision is processed so the particles will spray in the opposite direction of the ball's initial collision. We also set the particleSpeed of the emitter based on the collisionImpulse property of the SKPhysicsContact object. That makes the particles spray out farther in the few moments they emit if the ball hits the body harder.

We then call the custom category method on the spark, -rcw_dieOutInDuration:, that we wrote back in Chapter 3, *Explosions and Particle Effects*, on page 37, to make it easy to play particle emitters and remove them. Finally, we add the spark to the table.

That's it! The net effect is that a collision by the ball sprays out a brief puff of smoke based on the angle and how hard it hit. It's a small detail that adds to the frenzy and visual fullness of an action game like this. Give it a play and see what happens for yourself!

Next, let's finish the visual polish by adding a texture overlay on top of the table to cover up the dull bits and make it look more complete.

Covering the Table with a Textured Overlay

Yeah, skeuomorphism is passé for normal user interfaces. But for games, bring it on! We want to overlay a texture around the edges of the table to give a sense of depth and complete the illusion for the player.

Because SKSpriteNode objects can easily contain sprites with transparent areas, using one as an overlay is a snap. The graphics processor in modern iOS devices has more than enough horsepower to composite the overlay on top of the action going on underneath. This is the final effect that we'll get:

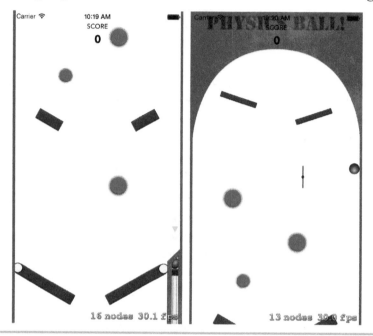

Figure 38—How the table overlay will look

We'll start by loading up the project at step 08-Polish/step07, which has the table-overlay.png file all ready to go in Xcode. Then let's open the RCWTableNode.m file and add these lines at the end of the +table method after the edge body is set up.

08-Polish/step08/PhysicsBall/RCWTableNode.m

```
bounds.path = bezierPath.CGPath;
bounds.physicsBody = [SKPhysicsBody bodyWithEdgeChainFromPath:bezierPath.CGPath];

➤ SKSpriteNode *overlay = [SKSpriteNode spriteNodeWithImageNamed:@"table-overlay"];
➤ overlay.size = CGSizeMake(320, 1246);
➤ overlay.anchorPoint = CGPointMake(0, 0);
➤ overlay.position = CGPointMake(0, 0);
➤ overlay.zPosition = 50;
➤ [table addChild:overlay];

  return table;
```

We create a new sprite node, overlay, with the image named table-overlay.png. After setting the size to fit properly over the table, we set the anchor point to {0,0}. Sprite nodes offer a special capability to let you shift their contents around with the anchorPoint property, relative to the value of the position property. The default value for anchorPoint is {0.5,0.5}, which means the sprite texture is centered on the position property. By setting the value to {0,0}, we shift the sprite texture so the position property is the bottom-left corner of the texture.

We also set the zPosition property of the node to 50 because we want this node to appear over all other nodes, except the score heads-up display. Remember that normally the node z-order is based on when you add nodes to the scene. Later nodes appear over earlier nodes. Because we want to override this, we explicitly set a zPosition. Anything over 1 would be sufficient; we just happen to be using 50 here. Pick a number that fits your use case.

If we were to run the game now, the heads-up display for the score would appear under the table when it scrolls as the ball skims up the side. We don't want that. We need to force the HUD to be drawn on top of everything else when we create it in the -setUpScene method.

```
08-Polish/step08/PhysicsBall/RCWMyScene.m
RCWHUDNode *hud = [RCWHUDNode hud];
hud.name = @"hud";
hud.position = CGPointMake(self.size.width/2, self.size.height/2);
➤ hud.zPosition = 100;
[self addChild:hud];
[hud layoutForScene];
```

Here we are setting the zPosition property to 100. Even though the RCWHUDNode and the SKSpriteNode for the image overlay are in different places in the child-node hierarchy, setting this zPosition property overrides any other ordering rules. This score heads-up display will always be on top.

Believe it or not, that's it! Because the table node contains all the action, adding this overlay is all we need to do. Run the game and see how beautiful it looks.

Depending on whether you tried it out on the simulator or a device, you might be doing a double-take right now. Running the game in the simulator with the table overlay will feel sluggish and a bit jerky. The frame rate drops as the simulated graphics hardware tries to keep up. Alas, that's the biggest limitation of the simulator. While most operations seem to go faster than on an actual device because of the Mac's more impressive hardware, graphics operations are actually *slower* than on a real device. An iPhone's native graphics pipeline has no trouble compositing this overlay on top of the fast-moving elements of the game.

This is a great moment to pause and reflect on how you go about game development. Tools like the simulator are a fine resource to get started quickly and whip up an idea. But when the time comes to do actual performance testing, do it on a real device. Ideally, you'll test on every device that you'll support, especially older models. The simple games like we've been building don't push the little machines very much, but when you start building your magnum opus and have hundreds (thousands?) of sprites flying around, you'll want to make sure that you're not causing frame drops and giving the player a sluggish experience. Test your game on older devices you plan to support, and adjust your strategy to remove unneeded nodes or cache things as much as possible when necessary.

That's it for the visual polish of the game. Before we wrap up the chapter, though, we need to quickly touch on some final adjustments to the UIKit portions of the app.

Locking the Game to Portrait and Removing the Status Bar

As you know, this is a book about Sprite Kit. We've talked about UIKit out of necessity to integrate with the rest of Apple's ecosystem for iOS applications. Before we can wrap up our discussion of the pinball game, we should make two minor changes to the app to get it ready for players.

First, the pinball game should not allow auto-rotation to landscape mode. It's meant to be played in portrait. But if the device is rotated while playing, the game will also rotate with it and look weird because of the way the scene scales to fill the width. It scales up because the scene's scaleMode property is set to SKSceneScaleModeAspectFill in the RCWViewController.m file by default. The scaling doesn't really matter for this particular game. We want to force the app to stay in portrait orientation.

Second, the iOS status bar is always visible, which doesn't make sense for a full-screen application like we have here. The process to hide the status bar changed from iOS 6 to iOS 7, so we have to tweak the Info.plist file and add a quick method call in the app delegate to make it go away.

In Xcode, we'll click on the top-level project item in the left-hand file list sidebar. Then we'll uncheck all the device-orientation checkboxes except Portrait, as shown in the following figure. That's all we need to do to force the app into portrait mode.

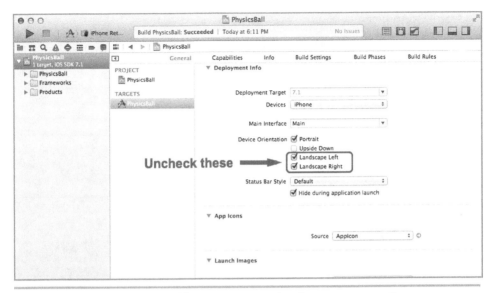

Figure 39—Checkboxes to remove landscape auto-rotation

Then, let's click on the Info tab in the top center of the window pane to view the Info.plist settings. We'll select one of the rows in the Custom iOS Target Properties list, and + and - buttons will show up. We'll click the + button to create a new key-value pair. Let's start typing the phrase "View controller-based status bar appearance" and choose it once the auto-complete figures out what we mean. We'll change the value column to NO, as in Figure 40, *Controlling status bar appearance*, on page 176.

That sets up the Info.plist file for this app with the right configuration in the bundle. But we still have to tell the status bar to hide when the app launches. Let's switch over to the RCWAppDelegate.m file and change the -application:didFinish-LaunchingWithOptions: method to look like this:

08-Polish/step09/PhysicsBall/RCWAppDelegate.m

```
- (BOOL)application:(UIApplication *)application
didFinishLaunchingWithOptions:(NSDictionary *)launchOptions
{
    [application setStatusBarHidden:YES];
    return YES;
}
```

That method call does the actual work to make the status bar go away. Now the game is truly full screen and an immersive experience.

Throughout this chapter, we've dabbled in a wide variety of techniques: detecting contact without triggering a collision, playing frame-based animations

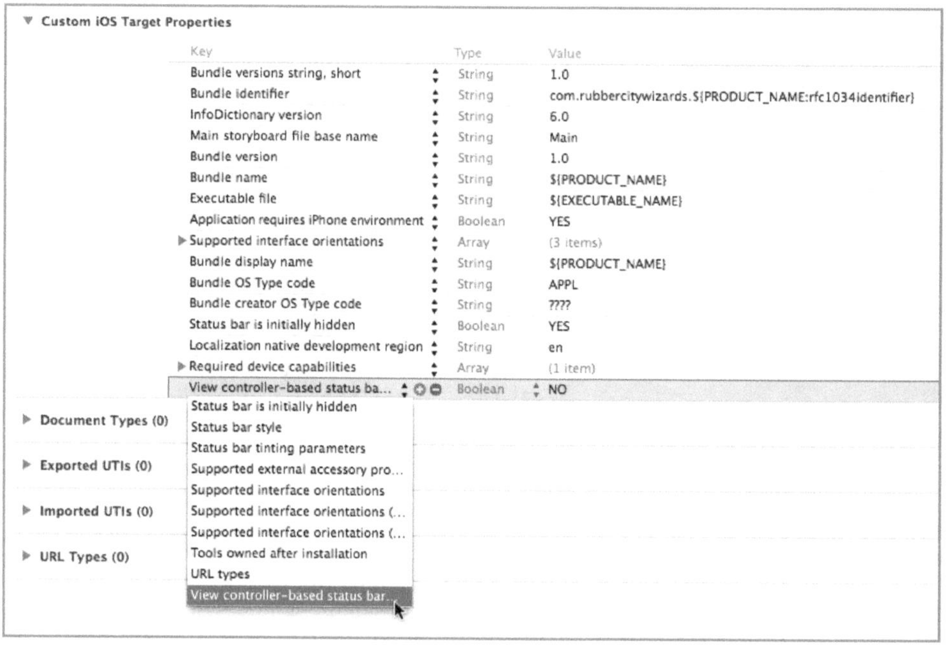

Figure 40—Controlling status bar appearance

efficiently, and using overlays to give the effect of depth and weight. At each point, we had a specific goal to achieve and looked into the Sprite Kit toolbox to find out how to solve it. It's the same process you'll repeat for your own games!

That's it for the coding examples in this book. You could do so many things to this game, such as adding an opening menu like we did for *Space Run* back in Chapter 4, *Menus and Cutscenes*, on page 53; giving the player only a limited number of balls; or maybe even using wacky physics and bumpers to give this pinball game a different feel. You've got the tools. Now run with your ideas!

Where to Go Next

Congratulations! You've made it through the projects in this book. You've grown your knowledge step by step and built two games with distinct mechanics. You've learned your way around the Sprite Kit APIs with the scene graph, actions, and many different node types. And you've seen some of the tradeoffs you have to make each step of the way to bring ideas to life.

We've barely scratched the surface of what is possible with Sprite Kit, but our goal (as your humble authors) wasn't to rehash Apple's excellent documentation. We wanted to help lead you through the thought process of building games. Given an idea, what would it take to get there? What compromises need to be made along the way?

We've got a few last points to leave with you before you venture off on your own. Take this as advice, not strict rules.

Reviewing the Game-Development Process

Now that you have two working Sprite Kit–based games running on the small device in your pocket, it can be easy to forget how it all started. Let's take a moment to review what we did in these pages, starting with the paper prototypes.

Prototype, Prototype, Prototype!

Back in *Preface*, on page vii, we first sketched out the ideas of *Space Run* and our pinball game. We drew rough images of what we wanted to see and listed key features we thought were most important for fun.

Note that these were not high-quality drawings. They were hastily scribbled on paper, just enough to get the point across. It's useful to get your ideas down in a sketched and temporary form that you're not attached to and that is easy to throw away. If you just sit down and start typing code but you discover later that the game idea isn't fun, the temptation to keep typing grows fierce. Indeed, we've all heard of (or lived through) projects that failed miserably because the team chose to ignore the signs of doom and kept going, hoping it would work out in the end.

The bottom line is that you can't type your way to fun. Draw the game out first. Set it in front of your friends, family, and colleagues and see what they think. Crinkle up the paper and draw it again. Try to get the essence of the game in front of them. It won't tell you everything, but you'll be amazed at the kinds of feedback and questions you can get from these quick sessions.

Take that feedback and start developing a larger plan of attack. Just because someone doesn't get it when you try to show the idea on paper, that doesn't mean you should abandon it. Being understood is just as important as the other person's ability to understand. Often, the push-back we get when we show prototypes helps us hone our ideas for the next time we ask for feedback. It helps us focus our efforts for when we actually start building.

What Are Your Goals?

So, the paper prototypes are finished, and other people like the idea. It's time to start building. Fire up Xcode and type, right? Well, not yet. Noodling around with Sprite Kit for fun is a great idea, but when you are ready to build a game, you need goals. In fact, so do your players!

Do you know who your audience is? Are they young? Old? Do they have fast reflexes? Think through the cognitive complexity of your game. Fast-moving shapes that you have to touch accurately with a finger don't work well for small children or older adults. The amount of information on the screen affects how much "fun" the player is having.

Does the game have a specific ending or goal for the player? *Space Run* and our pinball game are what are commonly called "infinite runner" games, where the goal is to get farther (either in distance or in points) than you did the last time. They don't necessarily have an ending. These games were chosen specifically to make it easy to discuss the technical parts of Sprite Kit without getting bogged down by narrative or character development.

Other games have a storyline where a character makes a progression through a series of challenges before facing the final challenge, or "boss" in a character-based game. These kinds of games are much more demanding to create because they are driven by the story and illustration.

You should definitely read Apple's discussion of an app definition statement.[1] Take time to decide what the game should do, and use that definition as a map to keep you from getting lost.

You Don't Have to Be an Artist

See the graphic assets and sound effects that came with the sample code for the book? The authors made those! Neither of us has much experience with illustration, but that doesn't matter. While you are working out the mechanics of your games, you don't need to perfect the visual parts. For most games, the mechanics are more important than the visuals.

The visuals do come into play, especially when it comes to characters and storyline, but as the recent spate of *Flappy Bird* clones has shown, the attitudes of players are fickle. Spending hours on your pixel-perfect rendering and awesome storyline does not guarantee a payoff.

That said, the visual element is important. At its core, *Angry Birds* is a physics game where you are throwing circles and triangles at squares and rectangles. It wouldn't be what it is without the comic characters. There is certainly a point where the visual and audible components contribute significantly to a game's feel.

Finding artists can be a complicated process. Start by looking through the variety of work and visual styles at sites such as Dribbble or deviantART.[2,3] These are great places to browse and find someone who might fit the style of game you're going for.

You can also go to Meetup and look up local illustration or game design groups.[4] Or go to a local college design department and ask around. Hang out with them and see what you find.

Bottom line, if you meet someone that you'd like to hire to work on your game art, treat that person like a professional. Those people are making a living off of what they are doing, just like you. Take them seriously.

For sound effects, it's hard to beat GarageBand as a fun tool to play with. The preset electronic instruments offer bloops and blips that are great to experiment with in your game. And as a bonus, GarageBand comes with gigabytes of royalty-free, liberally licensed music loops. Yes, it's easy to make

---

1. https://developer.apple.com/library/ios/documentation/userexperience/conceptual/mobilehig/Process.html
2. http://dribbble.com
3. http://www.deviantart.com
4. http://www.meetup.com

really cheesy audio tracks with them. But at the very least you can use them as filler to get the emotional effect you want from the music and replace them with something custom when you're ready.

We hope you are noticing a theme here. Don't fret about the graphics and music. It's very rare that they play a critical part of the game mechanics. Work out the details of gameplay first, using whatever you have around you. Polish it later.

Other Resources

We suggest some further reading to help round out your ideas in other areas. Game development isn't just about programming or sprites. Communicating visually is a fascinating and well-developed discipline, as you'll see in the following resources.

Apple's Documentation

When Apple introduced Sprite Kit, it included the most complete and useful set of documentation at launch day of any developer-focused product the company has ever shipped. Not only are their developer's guide and API reference excellent sources of information,[5,6] but there's an entire demo adventure game that you can try to explore novel uses of the API.[7]

That adventure game is *quite* advanced—far too advanced for a beginner to sit down and browse through without getting lost. But now that you've completed the process of growing your own games from idea to device through the Sprite Kit API, you've got enough experience to see what they've done and incorporate those ideas into your own games.

And, of course, don't forget to check out Apple's impressive library of videos.[8] The Sprite Kit introductions at WWDC 2013 are quite well done and show off special effects features, such as SKEffectNode and SKCropNode, that we didn't cover here.

The Big Picture

Because you want to build games, you must read this seminal work on game design and its impact on society, *Reality Is Broken: Why Games Make Us*

---

5. https://developer.apple.com/library/ios/documentation/GraphicsAnimation/Conceptual/SpriteKit_PG/Introduction/Introduction.html

6. https://developer.apple.com/library/ios/documentation/SpriteKit/Reference/SpriteKitFramework_Ref/_index.html

7. https://developer.apple.com/library/ios/documentation/GraphicsAnimation/Conceptual/CodeExplainedAdventure/AdventureArchitecture/AdventureArchitecture.html

8. https://developer.apple.com/videos/

Better and How They Change the World [McG11], by Jane McGonigal. She focuses on the academic side of games, treating them as performance art with positive social impact and not just as something that neurotic people use to escape from reality.

McGonigal's core thesis is that the components of games that make them fun and engaging can teach us a lot about how we could structure the challenges we face in our day-to-day lives. Whether it be home, business, politics, science, or religion, the way we state the problems we face has meaning. Games can help us frame our participation cooperatively with friendly competition to help us push each other in fun ways.

We, the authors, have seen this play out in our own work. Much of our recent work with games involves applications that help people with cognitive impairment. These are not consumer games with an in-app purchase. They are used in a variety of medical and research settings. But they affect people's lives by helping them cope with stress or injury and strengthen their mental muscles. Not every game needs happy birds or angry pigs to make a difference. We'd encourage you to reach outside of the normal commercial frenzy to see how games can improve the world around you.

Whether or not you agree with the specific prognosis McGonigal makes based on her research, it's a great starting point to see how games can make a positive impact.

The Design Process Itself

When you're ready to get down to the nitty-gritty parts of game design, you often need to look for inspiration and ideas. Or you can even walk through a process to generate those ideas for yourself! That's where these books can come in handy.

Level Up!: The Guide to Great Video Game Design [Rog10], by Scott Rogers, and *The Art of Game Design: A Book of Lenses [Sch08]*, by Jesse Schell, are great places to see how game designers organize their thoughts. Often we just need to put our finger on some vague idea in our mind. These books are chock full of vocabulary, examples, and more to help you firm up your idea into something you can describe to others and prototype.

When you are ready to break out of your shell and experiment with others, check out *Game Design Workshop: A Playcentric Approach to Creating Innovative Games [Ful14]*, by Tracy Fullerton. It helps kickstart the creative process in a group to help you with prototyping, play testing, and working with your tools.

Data Visualization

When thinking about how to display things in games, such as statistics for heads-up displays, or meters and puzzles, we recommend starting with books like *The Wall Street Journal Guide to Information Graphics [Won13]*, by Dona Wong, and *The Visual Display of Quantitative Information [Tuf01]*, by Edward Tufte.

These are not marketed toward game developers and designers, but the concepts are still useful. There's a lot of overlap between game design and informatics. Using well-researched resources like this can help you understand what your player experiences during your game and can give you ideas to present information in ways that communicate clearly and quickly.

Just Plain Fun

How can we suggest resources to help you build games without having a little fun? In case you didn't know, we are contractually obligated by the terms of the geek cards we carry to suggest the novel *Ready Player One [Cli12]*, by Ernest Cline. It's a fun read set in the future, where all commerce, entertainment, and even government takes place within an MMORPG.[9] When the creator of that MMORPG passes away, it triggers a quest with a grand prize for anyone who can decipher clues about the creator's life and obsessions.

The creator grew up in the 1980s and 1990s, so the only way to complete the quest is to know even the smallest detail of all the video games of that era. While the story is great on its own, the best part is the nostalgic trip down memory lane as Ernest recounts the experience of firing up the old 8-bit games—except this time, playing them has epic consequences that even your parents could get behind. If you were at all a fan of old video games, you'll enjoy this book.

Oh, and you'd better brush up on your *Joust*.[10]

Will I Hit It Big?

So, why are you trying to write games? The casual gaming market is fiercely competitive. We recommend that you leave your desires to get rich at the door. Game development is a rewarding process of creative action and collaboration. Enjoy it as you move through it.

---

9. http://en.wikipedia.org/wiki/Massively_multiplayer_online_role-playing_game
10. http://en.wikipedia.org/wiki/Joust_(video_game)

But if you really do want to try to make money building games, then think about another related creative industry: music. Millions of musicians are very skilled at what they do and perform regularly. They live on meager incomes, but they love what they do.

The most successful indie musicians know how to build a fan base. Folk wisdom in the indie crowd often says that all you need is 1,000 devoted fans to make an average living. These aren't just fans who say, "Oh, that's nice." These are the fans who go to all your shows when you're anywhere in a 75-mile radius. These are the fans who buy every piece of merchandise, from T-shirts to socks. They want the LP. They want to see you succeed.

How do you build a fan base like that? Ah, now you're asking the right question! If you want to make a living at building games, you need to think like an artist who balances personal creative vision with the whims of fans. It's hard work.

Bootsy Collins, one of the founders of funk music, told a story about his bandleader, James Brown, who once said that making music is 70 percent about the business and 30 percent about the music. We'd say the same thing about game development. If you want to succeed, plan to spend 30 percent of your time actually building and the other 70 percent working on the business side, promotion, shoulder-rubbing, and finances.

There's no guarantee of success, but focusing on the parts that generate buzz (making friends, building fans) increases your exposure. No one cares about the genius masterpiece crafted on a deserted island. Get your game out in front of people. Build up the momentum of a crowd so heavy with desire to see you win that they push you through the hardest of times.

Don't Forget to Play!

Sprite Kit is a great, ready-to-use framework for taking the ideas in your head and moving them around on iOS devices in two dimensions. We hope this little book helped you wrap your mind around how to apply it.

Don't just stop with this specific technical part of game development. Keep going and explore the world of game design and game theory. There's so much to learn as humanity grows and explores what technology can do to enrich society and give everyone opportunities. This is an unprecedented time when you have the opportunity to build amazing games on the small devices that live in our pockets.

Above all, have fun and don't forget to play!

Bibliography

[AD12]   Chris Adamson and Bill Dudney. *iOS SDK Development*. The Pragmatic Bookshelf, Raleigh, NC and Dallas, TX, 2012.

[Cli12]   Ernest Cline. *Ready Player One: A Novel*. Broadway Books, New York, NY, 2012.

[Ful14]   Tracy Fullerton. *Game Design Workshop: A Playcentric Approach to Creating Innovative Games*. CRC Press, Boca Raton, FL, Third, 2014.

[McG11]   Jane McGonigal. *Reality Is Broken: Why Games Make Us Better and How They Can Change the World*. Penguin, New York, NY, 2011.

[Rog10]   Scott Rogers. *Level Up!: The Guide to Great Video Game Design*. John Wiley & Sons, New York, NY, 2010.

[Sch08]   Jesse Schell. *The Art of Game Design: A Book of Lenses*. CRC Press, Boca Raton, FL, 2008.

[Ste14]   Daniel H. Steinberg. *iOS Storyboards: An Animated Tour for iPhone and iPad Developers*. Dim Sum Thinking, http://dimsumthinking.com/, 2014.

[Tuf01]   Edward R. Tufte. *The Visual Display of Quantitative Information*. Graphics Press, Cheshire, CT, Second, 2001.

[Won13]   Dona M. Wong. *The Wall Street Journal Guide to Information Graphics: The Dos and Don'ts of Presenting Data, Facts, and Figures*. W. W. Norton & Company, New York, NY, 2013.

Index

Test on iOS and add Sound

Learn how to do full-stack testing of your iOS apps and add live sound to all your apps.

Test iOS Apps with UI Automation

If you're an iOS developer or QA professional tapping through an app to reproduce bugs or performance issues you thought were solved two releases ago, then this is your book. Learn how to script the user interface, assert correct behavior, stub external dependencies, reproduce performance problems, organize test code for the long haul, and automate the whole process so the machine does the work. You'll walk through a comprehensive strategy with techniques using Apple's tools that you can apply to your own apps.

Jonathan Penn
(226 pages) ISBN: 9781937785529. $36
http://pragprog.com/book/jptios

Programming Sound with Pure Data

Sound gives your native, web, or mobile apps that extra dimension, and it's essential for games. Rather than using canned samples from a sample library, learn how to build sounds from the ground up and produce them for web projects using the Pure Data programming language. Even better, you'll be able to integrate dynamic sound environments into your native apps or games—sound that reacts to the app, instead of sounding the same every time. Start your journey as a sound designer, and get the power to craft the sound you put into your digital experiences.

Tony Hillerson
(196 pages) ISBN: 9781937785666. $36
http://pragprog.com/book/thsound

The Pragmatic Bookshelf

The Pragmatic Bookshelf features books written by developers for developers. The titles continue the well-known Pragmatic Programmer style and continue to garner awards and rave reviews. As development gets more and more difficult, the Pragmatic Programmers will be there with more titles and products to help you stay on top of your game.

Visit Us Online

This Book's Home Page
http://pragprog.com/book/pssprite
Source code from this book, errata, and other resources. Come give us feedback, too!

Register for Updates
http://pragprog.com/updates
Be notified when updates and new books become available.

Join the Community
http://pragprog.com/community
Read our weblogs, join our online discussions, participate in our mailing list, interact with our wiki, and benefit from the experience of other Pragmatic Programmers.

New and Noteworthy
http://pragprog.com/news
Check out the latest pragmatic developments, new titles and other offerings.

Save on the eBook

Save on the eBook versions of this title. Owning the paper version of this book entitles you to purchase the electronic versions at a terrific discount.

PDFs are great for carrying around on your laptop—they are hyperlinked, have color, and are fully searchable. Most titles are also available for the iPhone and iPod touch, Amazon Kindle, and other popular e-book readers.

Buy now at *http://pragprog.com/coupon*

Contact Us

Online Orders:	*http://pragprog.com/catalog*
Customer Service:	*support@pragprog.com*
International Rights:	*translations@pragprog.com*
Academic Use:	*academic@pragprog.com*
Write for Us:	*http://pragprog.com/write-for-us*
Or Call:	+1 800-699-7764

CPSIA information can be obtained at www.ICGtesting.com
Printed in the USA
LVOW02s1627170415

435046LV00005B/14/P